Israel's Emerging Constitution

Israel's Emerging Constitution

1948-51

By EMANUEL RACKMAN

New York 1955

COLUMBIA UNIVERSITY PRESS

First Published in Book Form 1955

PUBLISHED IN GREAT BRITAIN, CANADA, INDIA, AND PAKISTAN
BY GEOFFREY CUMBERLEGE, OXFORD UNIVERSITY PRESS,
LONDON, TORONTO, BOMBAY, AND KARACHI.

MANUFACTURED IN THE UNITED STATES OF AMERICA

Library of Congress Catalog Card Number: 54-12309

DEDICATED TO MY FATHER

from whom I learned the love of Israel

AND TO MY MOTHER

from whom I learned the love of humanity

Acknowledgments

In preparing this book I have had the invaluable assistance of Dr. J. C. Hurewitz of Columbia University. His is the major share of credit due for whatever value this study has; I alone am to be charged with its shortcomings. I am also deeply indebted to my beloved wife, Ruth, and to my dear friend, Moe Knieger, for their gracious goading of me to undertake the research and complete the manuscript. My loyal secretary, Mrs. Augusta Popolow, has patiently typed and retyped countless revisions of every chapter and section, and I am beholden to her beyond measure.

Introduction

The establishment of the State of Israel is regarded by many pious Jews as a miracle from Heaven. The least that anyone can say is that the achievement was well-nigh wondrous. Perhaps some day a genius of the mind and heart will write a book that adequately will record and evaluate everything that happened. This book purports to do much less. It deals with only one small phase of the miracle—the emergence of a constitution in the midst of war.

Apropos is the story told by the distinguished scientist, George Washington Carver, who discovered hundreds of new uses for the peanut. He once asked God to reveal to him the mystery of the universe. "George," said God, "the knowledge of that mystery is reserved to Me alone." Carver then asked God to reveal to him the mystery of the peanut. This God consented to do saying, "George, that is more nearly your size and I will reveal it to you." And so He did.

Perhaps I did dream of writing an inspired book that would reveal the mystery and essence of all that transpired in the early years of the world's youngest democracy. Perhaps I did want to write a comprehensive appreciation of the entire miracle. Instead, my book is limited to one small area—and perhaps even that area was beyond my size. It is, nonetheless, my offering to the men and women whose heroic accomplishments have won the admiration of noble people everywhere. Even when I am critical of what they have done, I seek to be constructive in my analysis. In no way do I intend ever to belittle the over-all grandeur of their historic feats.

The general reader may find the book too technical. Technical it is. Yet, there are many chapters and sections which can help all who are interested in Israel to acquire more authentic information about that country than now prevails in most circles. Had a formal constitution been formulated and approved by the Constituent Assembly, the preparation of this book would have been much simpler. All the pertinent data could then have been reported with relation to the specific articles and sections of the document. In the absence of such a text, however, it was necessary to resort to a different type of organization. The method chosen was to describe, historically and functionally, the several elements of which Israel's constitution is a composite and the background from which they emerge.

It is often said that Israel has no constitution. This is an error. The fundamental laws and practices that govern the operation of a state are its constitution, even if no specific instrument is thus entitled. As a matter of fact, the federal constitution of the United States is more than the document ratified in 1788: "While we still may properly enough refer to the document itself as 'the constitution,' in a larger and truer sense the constitution is the document *as enveloped* in a vast, living, changing complex of interpretations and usages."[1]

Israel does have a constitution, and this book purports to describe the making of that constitution in the first three years of the existence of the state. The three years include the period of the Provisional Government and that of the First Kneset. The First Kneset was really elected by the people to serve as a Constituent Assembly for the purpose of drafting a written constitution. Instead it changed its own status into that of a legislature and did not draft a written constitution worthy of the name. And, notwithstanding popular opinion to the contrary, there was opposition to a written constitution from political parties other than the religious ones.

[1] F. A. Ogg, and P. O. Ray, *Introduction to American Government* (New York, 8th ed., 1945), p. 38.

However, the United Nations General Assembly resolution of November 29, 1947, projected statehood and the drafting of a written constitution. This stimulated considerable thought and literary activity with regard to such an instrument. This thought and literary activity has already influenced the constitution and may yet influence future constitutional development. Since most of the writing was done by the political party heads and theorists, one must understand the parties, their backgrounds, their orientation, and their programs. That there are so many parties in so small a country has always confounded Americans. Yet one must be familiar with these parties if one is properly to understand even daily press reports from Israel. Cabinet crises, religious issues, even Israel's policies with respect to East and West are unintelligible except in the light of the party situation.

With respect to the religious problem one finds many Americans proposing that Israel adopt the American pattern of separation of church and state. They stubbornly refuse to consider the unique situation prevailing in Israel's legal order with regard to the marriages and divorces of her inhabitants—Jewish, Christian, and Muslim. It is a picture that must first be understood before panaceas can be offered. Furthermore, because of one provision in the United Nations' resolution on partition, the enactment of civil marriage and divorce in Israel might even precipitate a holy war in the Middle East. It is hoped that this book may clarify the picture and elevate the debate of Americans to the level of realism rather than fancy.

Moreover, Israel's military and territorial situation created unique constitutional problems. Israel, for example, encountered resistance to the nationalization of her army! Israel's immigration policy also precipitated new issues: Who is a Jew? What shall be the relationship between Israeli and non-Israeli Jews?

All of these problems must be of special interest not only to political scientists but to all who want to understand what the State of Israel has done, is doing, and will continue to do. Her economic and social problems may be her most important ones. She may have great need of American assistance in these areas. But her other more unique problems deserve at least the sympathetic understanding of her friends.

Needless to say, a description of the constitution of Israel could have been much briefer. However, I have essayed to write the history of the making of that constitution, attempting both an evaluation and a prognosis. Consequently, reference is made not only to elements that have already had constitutional significance but also to much that might yet influence further constitutional development. A prophet could have eliminated much. But one less prescient records and permits the future to reveal which events were passing shadows and which were the causes of lasting effects.

EMANUEL RACKMAN

Far Rockaway, New York
November, 1954

Contents

Israel's Emerging Constitution

CHAPTER I

Constitutional Antecedents

On May 14, 1948, the Provisional Government of Israel proclaimed its own existence and the independence of the new State. On that day also it was accorded *de facto* recognition by the United States. It had not, however, come into being—like Jonah's gourd—in a night. For more than a quarter of a century there had been a large measure of Jewish self-government in Palestine under the mandate. There were also cooperating organizations of world Jewry. Together they constituted what has been called the "Jewish quasi-government,"[1] from which there emerged many of the institutions and procedures of the State of Israel to date. The resolution of the United Nations General Assembly of November 29, 1947,[2] helped to condition later developments as did the Assembly's Palestine Commission which served in the early part of 1948. So did the advent of independence and the war for its retention. Nonetheless, the constitutional antecedents of the State of Israel are principally to be found in the structure of the World Zionist Organization, the Jewish Agency, and the Kneset Israel of erstwhile Palestine.[3]

[1] See J. C. Hurewitz, *The Struggle for Palestine* (New York, 1950), p. 38.

[2] United Nations General Assembly, *Official Records: 2d Sess., Resolutions* (Lake Success, 1948), Doc. A/519, pp. 131-50.

[3] For a good brief history of all three, see Z. Infeld, *The Jewish State in the Making*, issued by the Cultural Department of the South African Zionist Federation (Johannesburg, n.d.), pp. 3-42.

THE WORLD ZIONIST ORGANIZATION AND THE JEWISH AGENCY

The World Zionist Organization is a membership organization which was recognized in the mandate for Palestine[4] as "the appropriate Jewish agency . . . for the purpose of advising and cooperating with the [British] Administration" to develop the country, establish the Jewish national home, and advance the interests of the Jewish population in the land. In 1929, however, an enlarged Jewish Agency for Palestine was created. It consisted of non-Zionists as well as Zionists. The former were more interested in the establishment of the national home as a cultural and religious center than as a Jewish state. The main office of the enlarged Agency was in Jerusalem, and its Executive was responsible for the implementation of policies determined by its Council and Administrative Committee.

At the same time, the World Zionist Organization continued to function and even to grow. Its president automatically became president of the Jewish Agency, and at biennial congresses it elected its representatives to the Council of the Agency. At these congresses Zionist policy was also determined, and in interim periods decisions were made by its General Council or Actions Committee. In 1935 its Executive moved from London to Jerusalem. And since "the Zionists within the Jewish Agency were far more powerful than the non-Zionists, the members of the Zionist Executive, in their individual capacities as heads of various Agency departments, were able to execute the policy of the Zionist Organization."[5]

The Zionist organization and the Jewish Agency represented world Jewry's interests in the national home. But Palestine's Jews had, in addition, what was called the Kneset Israel.[6]

[4] Article 4. The text of the mandate is contained in Command Paper 1785 of Great Britain's Colonial Office, entitled "League of Nations: Mandate For Palestine" (London, n.d.), pp. 2-9, and in P. L. Hanna, *British Policy in Palestine* (Washington, D. C., 1942), pp. 162-69.

[5] Hurewitz, *Struggle for Palestine,* p. 41.

[6] Esco Foundation for Palestine, *Palestine: A Study of Jewish, Arab and British Policies,* 2 vols. (New Haven, 1947), I, 408-14.

Even before the first World Zionist Congress in 1897, many Jews had emigrated to Palestine with what was a Zionist motivation. Their number, however, was insignificant by comparison with the Jews who constituted the religious communities of Jerusalem, Safed, Tiberias, and Hebron.[7] The latter were in fact hostile to the new arrivals and their ideology, and were virtually excluded from whatever projects were undertaken to organize Palestine's Jewry before World War I.[8] However, after World War I there was created a statutory community—the Kneset Israel—to concern itself with Jewish affairs in the land. In 1928 its constitution received official recognition by the mandatory power. Still not all Jews participated. The rigidly fundamentalist Jews who were organized as the Agudat Yisrael declined participation even as they remained outside the fold of the World Zionist Organization. They would not cooperate with Jews whose nationalism was secular rather than religious or with Jews who flouted the traditions of Judaism. Moreover, they held the prophetic dream of Zion rebuilt to be one that would be fulfilled by divine intervention rather than by human effort.

THE KNESET ISRAEL

The regulations of the Palestine Government established the powers and functions of the Kneset Israel.[9] After describing the Rabbinical Council and Offices[10]—their constitution, jurisdiction, and maintenance—the regulations dealt with the Elected

[7] About 55,000 out of a total of 60,000 Jews in Palestine in 1900 lived in these cities. See M. Burstein, *Self-Government of the Jews in Palestine* (Tel Aviv, 1934), p. 4.

[8] *Ibid.*, p. 69. For an account of these early attempts to organize Palestine's Jewry, see *ibid.*, pp. 65-78.

[9] The full text is published in the *Official Gazette of the Government of Palestine*, No. 202, January 1, 1928, pp. 10-19. The amendments are found in the *Palestine Gazette*, No. 427, March 15, 1934, Supp. 2, pp. 218-20; *ibid.*, No. 663, January 28, 1937, Supp. 2, pp. 27-29; *ibid.*, No. 749, January 13, 1938, Supp. 2, p. 53; and *ibid.*, No. 843, November 24, 1938, Supp. 2, pp. 1520-21.

[10] The secularists would have wanted the order reversed. See Burstein, *Self-Government*, p. 166, n. 23.

Assembly (Asefat ha-Nivharim) and the National[11] Council (ha-Wa'ad ha-Leumi). The members of the Elected Assembly were to elect the members of the National Council annually and pass resolutions for the latter's guidance. They also were to grant the Council a budget for discharging delegated functions. Their term of office was three years.[12]

They were to obtain the necessary funds from members of the Kneset Israel through the local communities. However, the funds could be used only for specified purposes: education, relief of the poor, care of the sick, support of orphans, and the maintenance of the organs authorized by the regulations. The Elected Assembly could also approve regulations for the election or appointment of the Rabbinical Council and for the organization of the Rabbinical Offices.

The electoral law for the first Assembly following official recognition (though the third since its organization) was promulgated on March 1, 1930.[13] It provided for a general and direct election by secret ballot (para. 4). There were no qualifications as to property or sex, and representation was to be proportional and national, but not local. Palestine was deemed one electoral area (para. 5). Voters would vote for so-called party "lists" (para. 16). Usually these lists were chosen by the party machine rather than by party caucus, and a voter chose not a particular candidate but a particular party.[14] Voters could, however, delete names from the lists (para. 15 and para. 21). Only persons on the register of the Kneset Israel could vote (para. 6). The age requirement for voters was twenty, while candidates were to be twenty-five years of age (para. 6 and para. 7).

[11] The regulations used the term "General" Council, but this is an incorrect translation. See Burstein, *Self-Government*, p. 166, n. 22.

[12] This was later changed to four. *Palestine Gazette*, No. 663, January 28, 1937, Supp. 2, p. 27. However, the term of the Assembly elected in 1931 was extended till 1944.

[13] *Official Gazette of the Government of Palestine*, No. 254, March 1, 1930, pp. 142-45.

[14] Hurewitz, *Struggle for Palestine*, p. 42.

After the local electoral committees had reported to the central electoral committee, the total of all the votes cast was divided by 71. By the quotient thus obtained the list of candidates was divided. The integral number derived represented the number of candidates elected from the party list. The remainders in this arithmetic computation were used to determine the allocation of the balance of the seats still unfilled. These seats were assigned in order to the parties with the largest remainders until none were left. However, up to three days before the election, party leaders might have agreed among themselves as to how they wanted to combine their remainders of votes (para. 20). Moreover, seats had to be reserved for representatives of the Sephardic and Yemenite communities in proportion to their number on the register of the Jewish community rather than the number of votes cast for their candidates (para. 26 and para. 27). The number of votes cast for the parties of these communities helped only to determine the distribution of the seats reserved among the different parties of the Sephardic and Yemenite communities respectively (para. 28). This electoral law was the basis for the one approved by the State Council of the Provisional Government in 1949.

The membership of the Assembly, though 71 in 1930,[15] was increased in 1944 to 171. The National Council consisted of 23 members[16] to whom, as a body, were delegated the functions of the Elected Assembly between the latter's sessions. The powers of this Council were extended by an amendment to the regulations,[17] and later it was one of the groups from which the State Council of the Provisional Government of Israel was constituted. Actual administration of the community, however, was

[15] Representatives of the Local Councils were later invited to join the Elected Assembly. See M. Attias, *Kneset Yisrael be-Erez Yisrael* (Kneset Israel in the Land of Israel) (Jerusalem, 1944), pp. 73-78.

[16] This was later increased to 42. *Palestine Yearbook, 5706* (Washington, 1946), p. 177.

[17] *Palestine Gazette,* No. 427, March 15, 1934, Supp. 2, p. 219.

in the hands of the Hanhalat ha-Wa'ad ha-Leumi (National Council Executive) which the Council elected,[18] and with the Jewish Agency's Palestine section and the World Zionist Organization's Executive in Jerusalem it performed numerous functions of government.

The National Council was also actively concerned with Jewish organization on the local level.[19] The local units of the Kneset Israel were the Qehilot. In communities which were wholly Jewish, the municipality itself was such a unit. Where the population was mixed, there was a separate Jewish communal organization.[20] Often local interests took precedence over the national interest, and the influence of the Wa'ad Leumi in such situations helped to create national solidarity.[21]

ESTABLISHMENT OF THE PROVISIONAL GOVERNMENT

An examination of the three units of the Jewish quasi-government reveals that almost every function of government was performed by some department which might ultimately become a ministry in an independent, sovereign state.

The Jewish Agency Executive in Jerusalem in 1946 and 1947 had the following departments: Treasury, Political, General Secretariat, Agricultural Colonization, Immigration, Labor, Resettlement of Immigrants from Germany, Economic, Trade and Industry, Artisans and Small Trade, Technical, Statistical, Press, Delegates from the Diaspora, Information, Communication and Transport, Maritime and Fisheries, Youth Aliyah, Supply, and Housing. It also maintained an agricultural research institute

[18] This was authorized by an amendment to the regulations; see *ibid.*

[19] Some of the problems of local government in Palestine were set forth in a memorandum called "Local Government in Palestine," submitted to the United Nations Special Committee on Palestine on behalf of the Wa'ad Leumi in 1947.

[20] See B. D. Weinryb, *The Yishuv in Palestine* (New York, n.d.), p. 19.

[21] See Attias, *Kneset Yisrael*, p. 87.

station, an economic research institute, a relative research bureau, and the Bialik Foundation.[22]

By this time the Agency was a Zionist body for all practical purposes,[23] and it never again regained its original character as a mixed body of Zionists and non-Zionists with a semblance of right to speak for all Jews. But the Zionist Executive continued to function as well. In addition to offices concerned with its work outside of Palestine, the Zionist Organization had a political department in Jerusalem, as well as the offices of the major funds it had created—the Jewish National Fund and the Palestine Foundation Fund. The latter is the main financial instrument of the Jewish Agency.[24]

The Wa'ad Leumi's portfolios included Municipal Affairs, Qehilot Department and Rabbinical Institutions, Immigrants' Welfare, Education, Health, Social Service, Press and Information, Welfare for Discharged Servicemen and Auxiliary Police, *rapporteur* in recruiting matters, *rapporteur* on security questions, and Diaspora matters.[25]

The function of the Agency might be described as "dynamic." It involved immigration, land acquisition, and industrial development. The function of the Wa'ad Leumi was more "static." It fulfilled the educational, social, and health needs of the residents.

In some areas there was an overlapping of functions between the three constituents of the Jewish quasi-government. Yet it appears that when the Provisional Government of Israel was set up in 1948 the portfolios were not new. Nor were the personnel of either the State Council of the Provisional Government or the Provisional Government itself inexperienced.

The decision to proclaim independence was made on March 1,

[22] E. Schmorak, *Establishment of the Central Control Office of the World Zionist Organization and the Jewish Agency for Palestine* (memorandum submitted to General Zionist Council [Jerusalem, 1947]), p. 23.

[23] Hurewitz, *Struggle for Palestine*, p. 157, and p. 344, n. 4.

[24] *Palestine Yearbook, 5706*, p. 329.

[25] *Ibid.*, p. 181.

1948, by the Wa'ad Leumi. On March 23, the Wa'ad Leumi and Jewish Agency made known their plans for the Provisional Government, and on April 12 these plans were approved by the General Council of the World Zionist Organization, its policymaking body in intervals between biennial congresses. It was agreed that on the date of the termination of the mandate, an independent, sovereign state should be established. The State Council (first called People's Council) was to consist of 38 members, 13 of whom would constitute the executive branch—the Provisional Government. The members of the Council were selected as follows: (a) the 14 members of the Wa'ad Leumi Executive; (b) 11 Palestine members of the Jewish Agency Executive;[26] (c) the remaining 12 from those parties and communities which were represented in neither the Wa'ad Leumi nor the Jewish Agency. Dr. Chaim Weizmann subsequently became the thirty-eighth member.

THE UNITED NATIONS GENERAL ASSEMBLY RESOLUTION AND THE CONSTITUTION

The United Nations General Assembly resolution[27] of November 29, 1947, provided for the setting up of a Commission which would select and establish in each of the projected Jewish

[26] Members of the Wa'ad Leumi and the Palestine members of the Jewish Agency theretofore constituted the Wa'adat ha-Mazav (Committee of the Condition), which for several months before May 14, 1948, had been preparing for the new State (*Palestine Yearbook, 5709* [New York, 1949], pp. 73-75). The Minhelet ha-Am was the executive unit of the Wa'adat ha-Mazav. Even before May 14, 1948, it assumed powers and performed functions of government which the mandatory was abdicating (*Gilyon Minhelet ha-'Am, Zawim we-Hoda'ot* [Bulletin of the Minhelet ha'Am, Orders and Proclamations] [Tel Aviv, May 10, 1948], pp. 5-28). It had to make arrangements for the maintenance of government services and the defense of the land. It canvassed Arab, British, and Jewish civil servants as to their willingness to work for a projected Jewish state. It also established a school for diplomatic and administrative personnel and stepped up military recruiting (Hurewitz, *Struggle for Palestine,* p. 310).

[27] United Nations General Assembly, *Official Records: 2d Sess., Resolutions,* Doc. A/519, pp. 131-50.

and Arab states a Provisional Council of Government (Part I, B4). The Provisional Councils were to have broad authority over the areas under their control, subject to very few limitations by the Commission (Part I, B5). Not later than two months after the withdrawal of the armed forces of the mandatory, they were to hold elections to constituent assemblies which would be conducted on democratic lines (Part I, B9).

The election regulations were subject to the approval of the Commission *(ibid.)*. The resolution itself, however, specified that qualified voters should be persons over eighteen years of age who were: (a) Palestinian citizens residing in that state or (b) Arabs and Jews residing in that state, who, although not Palestinian citizens, had signed, before voting, a notice of intention to become citizens of such state. Women were given the right to vote and to be elected to the constituent assemblies. The Jews and Arabs of Jerusalem, which city was to have a special regime, might vote also, if they declared their intention to become citizens of the Jewish and Arab states respectively *(ibid.)*.

The constituent assemblies were enjoined to draft democratic constitutions (Part I, B10). Interestingly enough, while the United States and the USSR persistently differ within the Commission on Human Rights as to the meaning of "democracy,"[28] they agreed in the General Assembly on the character of the constitutions to be drafted in Palestine. They agreed that a parliamentary form of government was to be established with proportional representation, which already was the practice of the Knesset Israel. Furthermore, fundamental freedoms were to be guaranteed, including education, assembly, and association, and no limitations whatever were specified for any of them *(ibid.)*. Nor were economic rights mentioned. Apparently the Kremlin was more interested in the creation of a Jewish state for its effect upon the diminution of British control in the Middle East[29] than it was

[28] See J. N. Hazard, "The Soviet Union and a World Bill of Rights," *Columbia Law Review*, November, 1947, pp. 1095-1117.

[29] Hurewitz, *Struggle for Palestine*, p. 306.

in the consistency of its position on human rights in two different units of the United Nations.

The resolution included many provisions which were to be recognized as fundamental laws of the Jewish and Arab states (Part I, C). However, very little of the resolution has more than historic interest now. The boundaries it fixed for the Jewish state (Part II, B) were altered as a result of the war. Jerusalem was not internationalized. No Arab state came into being, and no economic union was established. The mandatory power did not cooperate, and the commission appointed was almost helpless. The Jewish state proclaimed its independence but the Constituent Assembly did not meet until nine months later, and no written constitution —as originally planned—has yet been approved.

Nonetheless, some contribution was made by the resolution and the Palestine Commission which served in the early part of 1948. The fact that the resolution called for a written constitution has been used on many occasions by the proponents of a written constitution for Israel as an argument in its favor. Furthermore, as will be seen in subsequent chapters, some proposed sections for a written constitution were based on the resolution, as were several laws approved by the Kneset.

THE PALESTINE COMMISSION AND THE CONSTITUTION

The Palestine Commission, which was to implement the United Nations General Assembly resolution, was indirectly helpful. It expected that the mandatory power would cooperate with it to the end that it might progressively take over the administration of Palestine and set up the provisional governments of the Jewish and Arab states. While it could not, for reasons beyond its control, fulfill its mission, it did meet some sixty-five times between January 9 and April 10, 1948.[30] These meetings, and the studies and correspondence they evoked, were revealing.

[30] United Nations General Assembly, *Palestine Commission Report*, Doc. A/532 (Lake Success, 1948), p. 4.

Of first importance was the submission on March 25, 1948, by Moshe Shertok, acting on behalf of the Jewish Agency, of a plan for the establishment of the Provisional Government of the Jewish state. This was the plan that was finally consummated. The Commission's recommendations on specific questions were sought,[31] and though these were never given, the Jewish Agency felt justified in continuing on its own, regardless of what the Arabs did.

Second, the Commission recognized that since the mandatory was surrendering its control at one time—on May 15, 1948—and not progressively, as had been anticipated by the resolution, the Jewish Agency had no alternative but to organize the Provisional Government in advance of that date, though such Government could not function earlier.[32]

Third, the organization of even a militia had to antedate May 15, for otherwise the new administration would be unable to maintain itself.[33]

Fourth, the preoccupation of the Commission with every type of governmental service—political, legal, economic, social—which it expected to take over from the mandatory, helped to make available considerable data which the committees of the Jewish Agency preparing for the Provisional Government of Israel were able to use.

Fifth, the correspondence of the Commission revealed that the Jewish Agency was representative of all the organized Jewish groups in Palestine. The Ihud and Agudat Yisrael were two exceptions. The former wanted only an opportunity to be heard by the Commission when it came to Palestine, and the latter wanted more members in the Provisional Government than Shertok's report indicated it would receive.[34]

[31] *Ibid.*, pp. 14-15. [32] *Ibid.*, p. 14. [33] *Ibid.*, p. 15.

[34] The writer was informed by Rabbi Y. M. Lewin, Minister of Welfare in the Provisional Government, that the Agudat Yisrael spokesman also expressed a preference for the portfolios of Immigration and Social Serv-

Thus it would appear that "the Commission was able, in close cooperation with the Jewish Agency, to make considerable progress in planning a Jewish provisional council of government,"[35] although it neither made nor executed any decisions.

SUMMARY

Israel's constitution was an organic development out of the Jewish quasi-government in Palestine. The Kneset Israel had a parliamentary form of government. Its executive was elected from its legislature, the Asefat ha-Nivharim. Therefore, when the United Nations General Assembly provided for a parliamentary form of government for the projected Jewish state, it provided for that which was already a fact. Moreover, the Executive of the Kneset Israel wielded most of the power. This condition never changed. In addition, the electoral system was well established before independence, and party control was already firmly in the hands of the party leaders.

With respect to the judiciary, the Kneset Israel was concerned with only one small unit—the Rabbinic courts. It had never interfered with their independence. With the advent of statehood, the entire judicial branch of the government came under the control of the new regime. Yet the form and the independence of the judiciary were preserved with virtually no change. The new state accepted the status quo.

Furthermore, as the Kneset Israel had not been sovereign in the mandatory period, so it was not altogether autonomous with respect to world Jewry, whose organizations were constituent parts of the quasi-government. And complete independence of the state vis-à-vis the British was to come sooner than complete independence with respect to the Jewish Agency and the World Zionist Organization.

---

ice, which would involve a minimum amount of compromise with its religio-political philosophy.

[35] Hurewitz, *Struggle for Palestine*, p. 313.

CHAPTER II

The Political Parties and Their Views on the Constitution

The State Council of the Provisional Government of Israel included representatives of all the Jewish political parties. Of these there had ever been an abundant crop in the Kneset Israel and the World Zionist Organization.[1] After May 15, 1948, however, there were few changes; therefore a description of them as of that date is generally correct for the period of the Provisional Government and the First Kneset.[2]

MAPAI

The Palestine Labor Party (Mifleget Po'alei Erez Yisrael) was and is the strongest of all the parties. In the last elections to the

[1] In the congresses of the World Zionist Organization, Palestine's Zionists were proportionately entitled to twice as many delegates as Zionists in the Diaspora. This helped to establish the Labor party as the leading party. For though the General Zionists were the strongest party outside of Palestine, Labor was the strongest in the land. Mizrahi, the party of those Orthodox Jews who remained within both the World Zionist Organization and the Kneset Israel, continued to be a minority party, but they enjoyed a balance of power on issues with regard to which the General Zionists and the Laborites were divided. Again one can find a portent of what happened in 1949 when Mapai and the United Religious Bloc joined to form a coalition government with the nonprogressive General Zionists in the opposition.

[2] The statistics given in this chapter were taken from a mimeographed study, made available by the Israel Consulate, called "Political Parties in Israel" and dated November 15, 1948. For additional information see *Zionist Newsletter*, No. 4, November 25, 1948, p. 8; *Parties in Israel:*

Asefat ha-Nivharim of the Kneset Israel, held on August 1, 1944, Mapai received 73,667 votes or 36.8 percent of the total of 199,-867.[3] In the State Council it was allotted 10 seats out of 38.

Mapai derives its strength from all sections of the Jewish working community of Palestine—from agricultural and industrial workers alike.[4]

As the majority party in the Histadrut (Israel's Federation of Labor), Mapai largely determines the policy of that organization, which is concerned both with the advancement of the interests of the Jewish working class and the establishment of commercial and industrial enterprises controlled by labor. Its policy has been defined as "revolutionary constructivism." Its labor outlook is, generally speaking, in line with that of the Second International, with which the party was affiliated. It does not accept an extreme view of the class struggle. It favors a measure of private enterprise in a controlled economy, and visualizes cooperation between capital and labor for the advancement of the social weal.

Both before and after the convening of the Constituent Assembly, Mapai's spokesmen gave expression to many diverse points of view on constitutional issues. David Ben Gurion, party leader and first Head of the Government, favored a written con-

---

Their History and Programs ("Zionist Organization of America Pamphlet Series," No. 6); Z. Infeld, *The Jewish State in the Making* (Johannesburg, n.d.); J. C. Hurewitz, *The Struggle for Palestine* (New York, 1950), pp. 44-50; *Survey of Palestine,* II (Palestine Government, 1946), 955-62.

[3] It should be noted that these elections were boycotted by the Revisionists, the General Zionists (Group B), and smaller right-wing bodies. Together these groups were deemed to have approximately 15 percent of the Jewish population supporting them. In the elections to the 22d World Zionist Congress held on October 22, 1946, Mapai polled 68,939 votes, representing 35.1 percent of the total of 196,189. In the elections to the Sixth Conference of the General Federation of Jewish Labor (Histadrut) which took place on August 6 and 7, 1944, the Labor Party obtained 57,135 votes, or 53.7 percent of the total of 106,420.

[4] Nearly all the members of agricultural settlements affiliated with the Hever ha-Qvuzot (Federation of Smaller Collective Settlements) and Moshavim (Cooperative Settlements) movements, and somewhat less than half of those in the Qibuz ha-Meuhad (Federation of Larger Collective Settlements) movement, supported this party.

stitution in 1948[5] and opposed it in 1950.[6] In the Kneset debate on the issue in 1950 his party divided.[7] It divided as well with regard to the issue of general national elections versus district or area representation. While its platform for the 1949 elections favored the former,[8] the opposing view was held by many members.[9] Mapai's spokesman in the State Council's Committee on the Constitution agreed that there were some advantages to area representation,[10] and for the elections to the Second Kneset this was a specific party proposal.[11] A unicameral legislature seemed to be the majority will, but there was support also for the bicameral idea.[12]

Though the party has one wing of religious workers (ha-'Oved ha-Dati), it generally favors a secular state. Nonetheless, it is not unanimously averse to the introduction of the jurisprudence of historic Judaism as the basis of the legal order.[13]

[5] David Ben Gurion, "le-Yisud ha-Medinah" (Upon the Establishment of the State), *ha-Po'el ha-Za'ir,* XIV, No. 13 (1948), 2.

[6] *Divrei ha-Kneset,* IV, 2d Sess., 117th meeting, 812-20.

[7] *Divrei ha-Kneset,* V, 2d Sess., 151st meeting, 1719-22, and *infra,* pp. 114-15. See also Natan Rotenshtreikh, "Huqah Le-Yisrael, ha-Higi'a Shatah" (A Constitution for Israel: Has Its Time Come?), *Molad,* No. 15 (Sivan, 5709: June, 1949), pp. 137-40. At page 140 the writer says: "Let us place 'Na'aseh' ahead of 'Nishma.' "

[8] See editorial in *ha-Po'el ha-Ziyoni,* XX, No. 15 (January 18, 1949), 2.

[9] Aryeh Shmuel, "Huqat ha-Medinah ha-Ivrit" (The Constitution of the Hebrew State), *be-Terem,* 4 Adar II, 5708: March 15, 1948, p. 13. In one Mapai publication another way to eliminate smaller parties was proposed. Each party nominating a list of candidates, or each candidate, should be required to submit a deposit which would be forfeited if the party, or candidate, respectively, did not get a specified minimum number of votes (Y. Bar-Shirah, "mi-Bayoteha Shel Parlamentariyut Yisraelit" [Of Israeli Parliamentary Problems], *Molad,* No. 11 [Shevat, 5709: February, 1949], pp. 267-72).

[10] *Wa'adat ha-Huqah Proceedings* (ha-Qiryah, 1949), Pamphlet I, p. 9 (hereinafter cited as *W.H. Proceedings*).

[11] *Divrei ha-Kneset,* IX, 3d Sess., 247th meeting, 1604-05.

[12] See Menahem Or, "ha-Histadrut ha-Ziyonit we-ha-Medinah ha-Ivrit" (The Zionist Organization and the Hebrew State), *be-Terem,* 4 Shevat, 5708: January 15, 1948, p. 46.

[13] See M. Zilberg, "ha-Mishpat ba-Medinah ha-Ivrit" (Law in the Hebrew State), *be-Terem,* 21 Shevat, 5708: February 1, 1948, p. 16. For a more realistic discussion of the same issue, see K. Hilv, "ha-Mishtar ha-

Meir Grabovsky, the party's spokesman in the State Council's committee on the constitution, opposed the granting of citizenship to Jews outside Israel. Such persons, he argued, would enjoy a privilege without any obligation to the State; they would possess an Israeli passport and make no contribution to the development of the land or its defense.[14] But, the view was expressed in a magazine edited by a party leader that Jews outside Israel should even vote for members of the Israeli legislature.[15]

Mapai favors the election of the president by the legislature. It also wants the role of the president of Israel to be like that of the president of France rather than the more powerful president of the United States.[16] However, there is support also for his direct election by the people and the broadening of his executive power.[17]

Generally it can be said that Mapai is not doctrinaire in its religious, social, political, and economic platforms. That helps to distinguish it from the other major labor party, Mapam.

MAPAM

The United Labor Party (Mifleget ha-Po'alim ha-Meuhedet),[18] which stands to the left of Mapai, came into being in January, 1948, as a result of the merger of ha-Shomer ha-Za'ir and le-Ahdut ha-Avodah Po'alei Ziyon.[19]

The merger, however, was hardly more than a federation. Both

Mishpati ba-Medinah ha-Ivrit" (The Legal Order in the Hebrew State), *be-Terem*, 21 Adar II, 5708: April 1, 1948, pp. 6-8.

[14] *W.H. Proceedings*, Pamphlet I, p. 8.

[15] Zev Rosen, "le-Mivneh ha-Medinah u-Mangenonah" (The Structure of the State and Its Machinery), *be-Terem*, Elul, 5708: September, 1948, p. 69.

[16] *W.H. Proceedings*, Pamphlet I, p. 8.

[17] Aryeh Shmuel, "Huqat ha-Medinah," *be-Terem*, p. 12.

[18] In the 1946 Zionist Congress elections the constituent parties of Mapam together polled 47,993 votes (24.5 percent of the total); at the last Asefat ha-Nivharim elections, 42,941 votes (21.5 percent); and at the Histadrut Conference elections, 40,799 votes (38.3 percent).

[19] The latter party had been established in 1946 by the merger of ha-Tnu'ah le-Ahdut ha-'Avodah (Movement for the Unity of Labor) and

groups retained their separate organizations, and party conferences always revealed the cleavage. During the Korean War it became apparent that in matters concerning the international situation there also was no unity. While ha-Shomer ha-Za'ir sought greater identification with the USSR, its partner in Mapam wanted strict neutrality between East and West.[20] Yet they were united in their opposition to the ever-growing bonds between Israel and the United States.

In the State Council of the Provisional Government, Mapam was allotted five seats. Its principal source of strength is the collective agricultural settlements: all the members of ha-Qibuz ha-Arzi (Federation of ha-Shomer ha-Za'ir Collectives) and over half of those of the Qibuz ha-Meuhad movements. Mapam also has a following among the urban workers and the intelligentsia. While Mapai espouses socialist doctrines of a reformist or gradualist variety, Mapam is dedicated to revolutionary socialism and seeks a greater measure of independence for the labor movement with relation to the state. The more radical attitude of the party on internal social issues also affects its political orientation in the international field. Moreover, it is militantly antireligious.

Its spokesmen in both the Provisional Government and the First Kneset favored the drafting of a written constitution.[21] They criticized the limited resolution adopted by the Kneset in June, 1950, with regard to the constitution,[22] arguing that since

---

the left Po'alei Ziyon party. Ha-Tnu'-ah le-Ahdut ha-'Avodah had seceded in 1944 from the Palestine Labor Party, in which it had theretofore formed a left-wing opposition.

[20] Ha-Shomer ha-Za'ir hailed Egypt's fight against Britain. See M. Sneh, "bi-Sfinah Ahat'—l'Olam Lo" ("'In One Boat'—Forever No"), *'Al ha-Mishmar,* IX, No. 2508 (October 19, 1951), 2, 6. Ahdut Avodah was more mindful of Egypt's war against Israel and her blockade of the Suez Canal.

[21] In the State Council of the Provisional Government, Nahum Nir-Raffalkes (one of its leaders) favored the adoption of a specific mandate to the Constituent Assembly to draft a constitution within a specified time (*Mo'ezet ha-Medinah ha-Zemanit Proceedings* [hereinafter cited as *M.H.H. Proceedings*], thirty-sixth meeting January 13, 1949, p. 9).

[22] See *infra,* p. 117.

the resolution specified no time limit within which the appropriate committee was to submit a draft of proposed chapters, Mapai had conspired with the United Religious Bloc to sabotage the declared intent of the Kneset.[23]

The party's platform with regard to the constitution reflected its ideology. It wanted the constitution to provide not only for the sovereignty of the State but for its independence.[24] Sovereignty might be construed to mean sovereignty with respect to subjects only. Mapam, however, wanted to preclude any subjection of Israel by other powers through economic or military commitments.[25]

It also wanted a completely secular state.[26] Furthermore the party wanted civil marriage and divorce for Jews and non-Jews.[27] It was very critical of Mapai because Mapai, by forming a coalition with the Religious Bloc, had deferred the Kulturkampf which such a reform would precipitate.[28]

Mapam did not favor a binational state, but regarded it as wishful thinking to assume that Israel would ever be uninational.[29] It asserted that Arabic should be a second language for all official purposes, not alone in areas where Arabs reside;[30] also that Christians and Muslims should be guaranteed complete equality, though only Jews should have the right to immigrate into Israel whenever they so chose.[31]

With regard to social and economic rights, Mapam wanted the constitution not only to describe them fully but also to require their implementation;[32] cooperative enterprise should be

[23] See editorial in *'Al ha-Mishmar,* June 15, 1950, p. 1.

[24] *W.H. Proceedings,* Pamphlet I, p. 14.

[25] For Mapam's criticism of Israel's receiving assistance from the United States, see editorial in *'Al ha-Mishmar,* February 26, 1951, p. 1.

[26] *Ibid.,* February 1, 1950, p. 1.

[27] See editorial in *'Al ha-Mishmar,* April 2, 1951, p. 1.

[28] Editorial, "be-Rei ha-Yamim" (Mirroring the Times), *'Al ha-Homah* March, 1949, p. 5.

[29] *W.H. Proceedings,* Pamphlet I, p. 15.

[30] *Ibid.* [31] *Ibid.,* p. 14. [32] *Ibid.,* p. 15.

favored in both agriculture and industry, and the nationalization of land, water, electricity, minerals, and oil should be set forth as ultimate goals.[33] Mapam was critical of the State's failure to tax capitalists more heavily.[34] It also opposed the vesting of too much authority in the executive[35]—particularly, one may add, when it was not represented in the executive. If the party itself were in power, one wonders how it could possibly fulfill its revolutionary program without a powerful executive.

THE GENERAL ZIONISTS

There are at present two General Zionist parties in Israel: the General Zionists (right wing) and the Progressives (left wing).

In June, 1946, the General Zionists A and B, previously separate parties, amalgamated to form the United General Zionist Party, which represented itself as the party of "integration." The General Zionists, Group A, represented middle-class interests (those of small farmers, petty traders, and artisans) as well as members of the professions. Their outlook in social matters was progressive. They favored close cooperation with organized labor but recognized the decisive role of capital, subject to state control, in the reconstruction of Palestine. In the last elections to the Asefat ha-Nivharim their list of candidates, headed by Yizhaq Gruenbaum, secured 4,723 votes (2.4 percent).

Group B of the General Zionists, on the other hand, was more outspokenly rightist. Its social outlook was largely determined by the industrialists, merchants, citrus fruit growers, and landlords, as well as by the various associations these people formed. The strength of Group B before its amalgamation with Group A cannot be stated accurately, since it was one of the right-wing

[33] *Ibid.*, p. 16.
[34] Editorial, *'Al ha-Mishmar,* March 30, 1951, p. 1.
[35] *Ibid.*, June 15, 1950, p. 1, and March 6, 1951, p. 1.

groups which boycotted the elections to the Asefat ha-Nivharim in August, 1944.[36]

When, in June, 1946, the United General Zionist Party was created its constituent elements survived within it as two organized factions. Real cohesion was never achieved, and the party's unity was ever precarious. Whatever unity existed was due to pressure from the World Confederation of General Zionists, which comprised both factions and their supporters all over the world. Because the composition of the State Council was influenced to some extent by party considerations in the World Zionist movement, in which the World Confederation of General Zionists was very influential, the General Zionists (including a labor arm, ha-'Oved ha-Ziyoni) were allotted six seats in the new body.

After the proclamation of independence, there developed a greater need for formulating a specific program in the social field, and, as a result, the rift between Group A and Group B became greater. The crisis culminated, in August, 1948, in the splitting of the party, and Gruenbaum's group (the former General Zionists A) formed the new Progressive Party.[37]

The General Zionist Party, which remained, can therefore be described as a right-of-center party, continuing largely, as far as its social outlook is concerned, the tradition of what was once Group B of the General Zionists. Only two of the six members of the State Council originally affiliated with it remained with the surviving group.

The Progressive Party, on the other hand, which came into

[36] In the Zionist Congress election in October 1946, the General Zionist Party in Palestine polled only 7,616 votes (3.9 percent).

[37] It should, however, be added that while almost all of Gruenbaum's followers joined the Progressive Party, Gruenbaum assumed an independent status. He remained in the State Council and in the Provisional Government as Minister of Interior, but in the elections for the Constituent Assembly he headed an independent list of candidates, none of whom was elected. In the 1951 elections he was included on the Mapam list.

being in September, 1948, represents a merger of 'Aliyah Hadashah, ha-'Oved ha-Ziyoni, and the left wing of the General Zionists, who, under Gruenbaum, had seceded from the United General Zionist party in August of that year.

'Aliyah Hadashah (New Immigration), numerically the most important constituent body of the Progressive Party, was distinctive before the fusion because of the common origin of its membership rather than its class affinities. Its members and supporters consisted overwhelmingly of immigrants from Central Europe who, because of linguistic and cultural differences, found it difficult to become assimilated into the existing political parties whose members were overwhelmingly East European. In 1942 they established a new political organization to put forward their specific demands and to ensure their adequate representation in the public institutions of Palestine Jewry.[38]

While the party had no clearly defined social policy, it generally took a progressive liberal stand on internal social issues. Its members and supporters were drawn from various classes, but the middle-class element predominated. 'Aliyah Hadashah was allotted one seat in the State Council.

Whereas both 'Aliyah Hadashah and Gruenbaum's supporters had been composed mainly of middle-class elements, ha-'Oved ha-Ziyoni (Zionist Worker), the third partner, had been a workers' party. It had stood for the unity of labor and its members belonged to the Histadrut. However, unlike the two major parties of the Histadrut, Mapai and Mapam, ha-'Oved ha-Ziyoni had been nonsocialist; it rejected the concept of the class struggle, claiming that all class interests had to be subordinated to the supreme national aim.

A number of agricultural settlements, collective and cooperative, were affiliated with the party, and they constituted its main-

[38] In the 1946 Zionist Congress elections, 'Aliyah Hadashah obtained 12,055 votes (6.1 percent) and in the last elections to the Asefat ha-Nivharim, 21,403 votes (10.7 percent).

stay. Whatever following ha-'Oved ha-Ziyoni had in the urban centers came mainly from white-collar workers and professional men.[39] This party was allotted one seat in the State Council (from among the six allocated to the General Zionists).

To sum up, the Progressive Party can be classified as a moderately left-of-center party.[40] While middle-class elements, largely of Central European origin, form the bulk of its members and supporters, it also has some support from workers. Progressive in its social outlook, the party stands for close cooperation with organized labor. White-collar workers among its members belong to the Histadrut (where they are organized in a special section under the name of ha-'Oved ha-Ziyoni). The party, upon coming into being, held four seats in the State Council. Yizhaq Gruenbaum also had a seat in the Council, but after August, 1948, he was associated with neither the Progressive nor General Zionist parties.

With regard to constitutional issues, the General Zionists and the Progressives generally hold the same views. Both want a written constitution, and in the Committee on the Constitution of the State Council both were represented by Yizhar Harari, whose resolution favoring a written constitution received Kneset approval on June 13, 1950.[41] He recommended a brief constitution that would set forth only general principles,[42] since a constitution too specific gives rise to many unintended inferences. The omissions can then become the subject of extensive interpretation. Of all France's constitutions, that of 1875—the shortest—enjoyed the longest life.

[39] In the 1946 Zionist Congress elections, ha-'Oved ha-Ziyoni polled 3,345 votes (1.7 percent); in the last Asefat ha-Nivharim elections, 3,693 votes (1.8 percent); and in the elections to the Sixth Conference of the Histadrut, 3,066 (2.9 percent).

[40] So serious is the cleavage between the Progressive Party and the General Zionists that the former were in the Coalition Government of 1949-51 while the latter were in the opposition!

[41] *Divrei ha-Kneset,* V, 2d Sess., 151st meeting, 1722.

[42] *W.H. Proceedings,* Pamphlet I, p. 9.

The General Zionists and Progressives both prefer a bicameral legislature,[43] feeling that a second house helps to avoid errors in legislation. Even if the additional house were not to be equal in power to the first, its influence would be invaluable; even delays can often be helpful. They do not feel that the simple fact of Israeli disdain for such groups as the British House of Lords should preclude the favorable consideration of a bicameral legislature, for such a house can also be democratic in character and give fair representation to all the political parties. It has been proposed that such a house might consider legislation only after its passage by the more popularly elected body, and have only the power to refer it back with recommendations for final passage. The parties conjecture that this upper house might be particularly helpful if it were to be constituted from among persons not subject to strong pressures from their respective party organizations. Their judgments would, in such a case, be more objective and would more correctly reflect the general welfare. The body might include past presidents of the State, or persons unanimously elected by the lower house in recognition of distinguished public service, or prominent persons who would hesitate to let themselves be nominated for election to office by popular vote.

These parties also agree that while the president should have powers comparable to those of the president of France, the executive branch of the Government should be truly powerful and not too easily removed by the legislature.[44] The Head of the Government should have the power to dissolve the legislature and call for a new election.

[43] *Ibid.*, p. 11. See also Meir Avner, "'Al ha-Haza'ah bi-Dvar ha-Behirot le-Veit ha-Nivharim" (On the Proposal with regard to Elections to the Legislature), *ha-Arez*, 12 Tishrei, 5709: October 15, 1948, p. 3.

[44] *W.H. Proceedings*, Pamphlet I, p. 12. See also M. Kramer, "'Al Huqat Yisrael" (On Israel's Constitution), *ha-Arez*, 20 Elul, 5708: September 24, 1948, p. 2. Kramer favors broader powers for the president to avoid parliamentary crises. He also recommended the popular election of the president.

The General Zionists and Progressives also favor measures to reduce the number of parties,[45] though such measures might adversely affect the continuance of the Progressives as an independent party.[46] They prefer district representation to national representation, or perhaps a compromise whereby one half of the legislators is elected at large by the method of proportional representation while the other half is elected from legislative districts.[47] The existing system of proportional representation, they feel, has helped to multiply parties and should be altered.[48] The number of signatures required on the parties' petitions to nominate candidates should be increased, and parties that fail to receive a specified minimum percentage of the total vote cast should have all the ballots in their favor cancelled.[49] In addition, the evils of the party system should be eliminated from the civil service.[50]

Even the Progressives favor constitutional guarantees with regard to the private ownership of property and free enterprise. They feel that since Israel has no big business or vast accumulations of wealth there is no need for a socialist revolution. The worker and the farmer are free in Israel. Furthermore, though it appears paradoxical, the General Zionists favored the nationalization of industry and labor in areas where Mapai opposed it.

[45] S. Gepstein, "Behirot we-Demoqratiah" (Elections and Democracy), *ha-Boker,* 15 Av, 5708: August 20, 1948, p. 3.

[46] The party apparently changed its mind in the Second Knesset.

[47] *W.H. Proceedings,* Pamphlet I, p. 12. See also Avner, " 'Al ha-Haza'ah," *ha-Arez,* p. 3, and Kramer, " 'Al Huqat Yisrael," *ha-Arez,* p. 2.

[48] A. Landsberg, "ha-Tnu'ah ha-Progresivit" (The Progressive Movement), *ha-Arez,* 10 Marheshvan, 5709: November 12, 1948, p. 3. It was argued that the system of proportional representation perpetuated the bureaucracy and prevented the election of outstanding personalities; its abolition would also make for closer contact between the individual citizen and his government.

[49] Editorial, "mi-Yom le-Yom" (From Day to Day), *ha-Arez,* 10 Marheshvan, 5709: November 12, 1948, p. 2.

[50] S. N. Eisenshtadt, "le-Darhei Binyan Mangenon ha-Memshalah" (On Ways of Establishing State Machinery), *ha-Arez,* 19 Tishrei, 5709: October 22, 1949, p. 3.

For example, they wanted housing projects and labor exchanges nationalized, while Mapai favored their control by the Histadrut.[51]

With regard to the role of religion in the state the parties generally maintained a middle-of-the-road position after stating that, because of the historic connection between Judaism and the Jewish people, it is impossible to conceive that Judaism should not be mentioned in the constitution. They would assure maximum freedom of conscience, even though the religious festivals should be national holidays and the laws of Judaism should, to a limited extent, enjoy recognition.[52] Yet civil marriage ought to be made possible.[53] Furthermore, there should be a unified educational system.[54]

MIZRAHI AND HA-PO'EL HA-MIZRAHI

These parties sought to establish the state of Israel in accordance with the religious precepts of Judaism.

The difference between the two groups lay in their social outlook. The attitude of Mizrahi on internal social issues was largely determined by the fact that its members were drawn almost entirely from the middle-class element. When the World Zionist Organization decided to engage in educational work in Palestine and the Diaspora, the party was formed by people who feared that the schools to be established would become secularist in character and that the nationalist ideology to be propagated would have nonreligious foundations.

[51] See "Labour Exchange Bill and the Histadruth," *Israel Economist*, VI, No. 2 (February, 1950), 37, and "Why In Opposition," *Inside Israel*, August, 1950, p. 5.

[52] *W.H. Proceedings*, Pamphlet I, pp. 12-13. See also M. Or, "ha-Mishpat bi-Mdinat Yisrael" (Law in the State of Israel), *ha-Boker*, 29 Elul, 5708: October 3, 1948, p. 14, favoring a limited use of Jewish law in the legal order.

[53] K. Hilv, "Dat u-Medinah" (Religion and State), *ha-Boker*, 15 Av, 5708: August 20, 1948, p. 3.

[54] Editorial, "Bayot ha-Hinukh" (The Problems of Education), *ha-Boker*, 20 Elul, 5708: September 24, 1948, p. 2.

The ha-Po'el ha-Mizrahi (Mizrahi Worker) was composed almost exclusively of Orthodox working-class elements. In addition to being a political party, it fulfilled many functions which the Histadrut performed for its members, such as finding employment and paying benefits in times of distress. Though there is now some cooperation between ha-Po'el ha-Mizrahi and the Histadrut,[55] ha-Po'el ha-Mizrahi was founded in 1921 as the Mizrahi Labor Federation by a group of workers who rejected the secular Histadrut. A number of collective and cooperative agricultural settlements, consisting entirely of Orthodox members, are affiliated with the party.[56]

There was some coordination of activities by the Mizrahi and ha-Po'el ha-Mizrahi on religious and cultural issues through the Merkaz 'Olami (World Center) movement in Jerusalem. At periodic conferences of the Merkaz 'Olami the two groups determined how they would allocate among themselves monies received from the United Jewish Appeal in the United States. Each of the parties, however, maintained a separate world-wide federation of its sympathizers. Together they were allotted five seats in the State Council.

With regard to the constitution, Mizrahi and ha-Po'el ha-Mizrahi agreed on most issues except economic ones. They maintained that religious bonds united Jews of the present with Jews of the past, as well as Jews in Israel with those outside. Jews in Israel did not feel that they were establishing a new nation. They felt rather that they were reconstituting themselves as a nation which already had an honored past. And they further felt a responsibility to Jews outside of Israel. The bonds that gave birth to these sentiments were and still are religious in character.

[55] Ha-Po'el ha-Mizrahi members are, for instance, entitled to use the services of the Histadrut's Sick Fund.

[56] In the elections to the 1946 Zionist Congress, the Mizrahi in Palestine secured 5,238 votes (2.7 percent), and in the elections to the Asefat ha-Nivharim, 7,752 votes (3.9 percent). In the same Congress elections, ha-Po'el ha-Mizrahi in Palestine polled 19,176 votes (9.8 percent), and in the elections to the Asefat ha-Nivharim 19,372 votes (9.7 percent).

Therefore they argued that the constitution could not ignore Judaism. If Israel did not take a positive stand on Judaism, Jews in America might even assimilate altogether. Consequently the state should be prevented from doing anything inconsistent with Judaism, thereby holding at bay assimilation abroad.[57]

Both parties asserted that traditional Jewish law should become the basis for the civil and criminal law of the state.[58] If civil marriage were introduced, and with it the legalization of marriages between Jews and non-Jews, then assimilation outside of Israel would be accelerated, and within Israel there would be two groups of Jews, one of which would refuse even to intermarry with the other.[59] The school system, however, could not be unified. To secularize education and to allow for an hour of religious instruction is to interfere with the freedom of conscience of Jews who feel that all of one's education must have a religious character. Their rights must be safeguarded too.[60]

The parties, however, before 1950, did not indicate any opposition to a written constitution. Apparently they saw nothing inconsistent between their loyalty to the Torah—the totality of Jewish law, oral and written—and the preparation and ratification of a written constitution for the new State. As a matter of fact, they conceded that such a constitution was necessary to establish the powers of the president, Government and Kneset.[61] At best they wanted decisions with regard to the role of religion in the State deferred,[62] until they could make substantial gains and then undertake to strengthen the State's fulfillment of Judaism. It was because of the other parties in the United Religious Bloc that in 1950 they changed their stand on a written constitution.[63]

[57] *W.H. Proceedings*, Pamphlet I, pp. 18-19.

[58] *Ibid.*, p. 20. [59] *Ibid.* [60] *Ibid.*

[61] N. Katzburg, " 'Al ha-Huqah li-Mdinat Yisrael" (On the Constitution for the State of Israel), *Sheluhot*, No. 6 (Av, 5709), pp. 10-12.

[62] *Ibid.*

[63] M. Una, "mi-Saviv ha-Kneset bi-Shelat ha-Huqah" (About the Kneset on the Issue of the Constitution), *Netiva*, 26th year, No. X, pp. 2-4.

AGUDAT YISRAEL

This is another religious party, one which, unlike the Mizrahi and ha-Po'el ha-Mizrahi, had never become affiliated with the World Zionist Organization, the Jewish Agency, or the Kneset Israel.

In recent years, however, a marked change has come about in the attitude of the party. In connection with the United Nations' deliberations on the future of Palestine, the Agudat Yisrael collaborated with the Jewish Agency and supported its fight for the establishment of the Jewish State. When, on May 14, 1948, the State of Israel came into being, the Agudat Yisrael joined the State Council, in which it was allotted three seats.

The majority of Agudat Yisrael's supporters are to be found in the Yeshivot—the theological schools. Workers who favored their point of view formed a party called Po'alei Agudat Yisrael (Agudat Yisrael Workers).[64] A few new collective agricultural settlements are affiliated with the latter group.

There are no accurate figures for the membership of Agudat Yisrael, but it is estimated that between 6,000 and 7,000 voters participated in the elections to the all-Palestine conference of the party, held in 1944.[65]

In November, 1948, the Mizrahi, ha-Po'el ha-Mizrahi, Agudat Yisrael, and Po'alei Agudat Yisrael concluded an agreement providing for the establishment of a United Religious Bloc for the elections to the Constituent Assembly.

Despite the appearance of unity, however, the constituent parties of the Bloc held widely divergent political and religious philosophies, as will be indicated in subsequent chapters.[66] Together they favored a greater role for religion in the state, but Agudat Yisrael regarded a written constitution as a negation of

[64] One of the three representatives of the party in the State Council was a member of this body.

[65] See mimeographed study referred to *supra*, p. 15, n. 2.

[66] *Infra*, Chapter XIII.

the fact that the Torah is Israel's constitution, requiring nothing additional.[67] They insisted that if there had to be a written constitution, it too should provide for the centrality of the Torah in the State's existence.[68] Judaism and its rituals should be more than a matter of individual conscience, though all non-Jewish religious communities might enjoy full freedom in such matters.[69] The government itself, however, should observe the rituals even in the exercise of functions such as granting permits for import. The government should also be enjoined from committing any offense against Jewish canon law in any of its activities, and the rabbinical institutions should be recognized as the highest authority in all matters pertaining to such religious problems.[70]

With regard to civil law, they maintained that the ultimate acceptance of the totality of Jewish civil law should be the goal. In the interim, however, all matters pertaining to the personal status of Jews—without exception—should be under the jurisdiction of the rabbinical courts, regardless of the citizenship of the Jew. In the matter of civil claims, a claimant should have the choice of suing either in a civil or rabbinical court and the judgments of the latter should be as binding as those of the former.[71]

They also asserted that the government should be required to provide education with due regard for the cultural and religious demands of the different groups in the land.[72]

As far back as 1937 one of Agudat Yisrael's leaders, Dr. Yizhaq Breuer, prepared a memorandum[73] with regard to a proposed constitution. It called for the ineligibility of any person to hold public office unless he was an observing Jew.[74] It called also for a prohibition against the use of the prayer book of liberal

[67] *W.H. Proceedings*, Pamphlet I, p. 22. [68] *Ibid.*
[69] *Ibid.*, p. 23. [70] *Ibid.* [71] *Ibid.* [72] *Ibid.*
[73] This memorandum, and others prepared by party leaders, are published in a pamphlet edited by Dr. Isaac Lewin, *Material for the Preparation of a Constitution for the Jewish State on a Religious Basis* (New York, 1948).
[74] *Ibid.*, p. 9.

Jews.[75] These are but two of many illustrations that indicate how nondemocratic were its proposals for the State. Nevertheless, the party had seen fit in recent years to cooperate with the Jewish Agency and to participate in the Provisional Government and the First Kneset. Its record in the Second Kneset may portend a reversion to its earlier philosophy.

Mizrahi's proposals, on the other hand, were always more conciliatory to the secularists,[76] and the ideological differences between the religious parties did come to the fore in the 1950 debate in the Kneset with regard to the constitution.[77] In the Second Kneset the split was violent on the issues of education and the conscription of women for labor.

REVISIONIST PARTY AND TNU'AT HA-HERUT

There is no material difference between the political and social programs of these two parties. Both have stood at the extreme right, been outspokenly antilabor, and propagated a nationalist ideology which called for conquest and territorial expansion. Their separate existence can only be explained by reference to their past.

The Revisionist Party,[78] which had always opposed the official Zionist leadership and charged it with too much cooperation with Britain's anti-Zionist policy, was the parent movement of the Irgun Zvai Leumi, a military force which acted independently of the Haganah, the illegal Jewish defense establishment that had the support of the Kneset Israel. The founders and the original members of the Irgun had all come from Revisionist ranks and considered that party as their representative in the political field. In the course of time, however, a rift developed between the two groups, with the Irgun seeking to free itself from the political control of the Revisionists and to gain independence in determin-

[75] *Ibid.* [76] *Ibid.*, pp. 28-30.

[77] See Una, "mi-Saviv ha-Kneset," *Netiva*, pp. 2-4.

[78] For about a decade after its organization in 1924 it remained within the fold of the World Zionist Organization. It returned again in 1946.

ing the course of its terrorist activities. There developed a continuous conflict between Menahem Beigin, leader of the Irgun, and the veteran leaders of the Revisionist Party. But the illegal military force could not openly enter the political arena before May 14, 1948. Therefore the sympathy which this terrorist group enjoyed among certain sections of the Jewish public could find no political outlet other than support for the legal Revisionist Party. This partly accounts for the fact that at the 1946 Zionist Congress elections the Revisionists secured a comparatively large number of votes (26,964, or 13.7 percent of the total). When the state was established, the party was allotted three seats in the State Council.

In June, 1948, however, Beigin launched the Tnu'at ha-Herut (Freedom Movement), declaring it to be the political successor of the Irgun. As this movement proclaimed its intention to engage in party activities and to stand for elections to the Israeli Constituent Assembly, the Revisionists found themselves confronted with the task of clarifying their relationship with Beigin's new party. On this issue a sharp controversy developed among the Revisionists, and at the national party convention held in September, 1948, an open split occurred. Defying the counsel of the veteran leaders, among them the party's three representatives in the State Council, the great majority of the delegates decided to break away from the Revisionists and to join the Tnu'at ha-Herut. Subsequent attempts to settle the differences between the two groups failed, and both offered separate lists of candidates in the elections for the Constituent Assembly. Only the Herut party, however, succeeded in electing any of its nominees. In May, 1949, an attempt was made to achieve the world-wide unity of Revisionists by organizing an "Igud" (federation). It led, however, to the liquidation of the Revisionist party in Israel.[79]

The members of the Herut party want constitutional guaran-

[79] M. Grossman, "Unity in Revisionist Ranks," *Zionist Record,* XLIII, No. 1384 (February 2, 1951), 21.

tees regarding private property and free enterprise.[80] They also want the constitution to avoid any implied waiver of any part of the whole of historic Palestine, notwithstanding the United Nations General Assembly resolution and British "faits accomplis" between the two world wars.[81] They also favor district representation, popular election of the president, and compulsory military service.[82]

ISRAELI COMMUNIST PARTY

At the extreme left stood the Communist Party, the only one with a mixed Arab-Jewish enrollment, which prompted it to regard itself prior to 1948 as the only truly Palestinean party though it was outlawed by the Palestine Government. Its attitude toward Zionist aspirations and demands had always conformed with the official policy of the USSR on Palestine.[83] When in 1947 the Soviet delegate to the United Nations General Assembly favored the establishment of a Jewish State in Palestine, the Palestine Communist Party followed suit. The party also welcomed the Assembly's decision of November 29, 1947 to partition Palestine into two independent states—one Jewish and one Arab.

In the last elections to the Asefat ha-Nivharim the party gained 3,948 votes (or just under 2 percent). Not being affiliated with the Zionist Organization, the Communist Party did not take part in the Zionist Congress elections. The members of the party belonged to the Histadrut. The party as such did not, however, participate in the last Histadrut Conference.

The party was allotted one seat in the State Council, and in November, 1948, formed itself into the Israeli Communist Party. The Israeli Communists have endeavored to join forces with Mapam, but Mapam has consistently demanded their formal

[80] *W.H. Proceedings*, Pamphlet I, pp. 6-7.
[81] *Ibid.* [82] *Ibid.*
[83] For an excellent description of its schizophrenia, see A. Hiram, "The Communist Party of Israel," *Jewish Frontier*, XVII, No. 7 (July, 1951), 14-19.

acceptance of the fundamental principles of Zionism as a prerequisite for negotiations.

Shortly after the elections of 1949, one of the deputies elected, Eliezer Preminger, was "purged" from the party and became the leader of a new party, the Hebrew Communists. On August 15, 1949, he announced in the Kneset that this new party had merged with Mapam.[84]

The Communist party is the one that wants the Constitution to fulfill every provision of the United Nations General Assembly resolution.[85] It favors proportional representation on a national basis.[86] It also favors greater protection for the Arab minority—including the granting of citizenship to Arabs who were inhabitants of Israel as of the date that the British mandate terminated.[87]

OTHER PARTIES

In addition to the parties enumerated, there are various small groups in Israel which, though not parties in the usual sense of the word, engage in political action and propose their own candidates in the elections. These groups have as their principal purpose the safeguarding of the special interests of their members; in one case the special interests of women—equal rights.

Foremost among these groups is the Representation of Sephardic (Oriental) Jews, which was represented in the State Council, as were the Yemenites and the WIZO (Women's International Zionist Organization). Each had one seat.

EVALUATION

The World Zionist Organization and its parties were European in origin. That accounts in part for their almost complete commitment to the parliamentary form of government and the dearth

[84] *Divrei ha-Kneset,* II, 1st Sess., 32d meeting, 1358.
[85] *W.H. Proceedings,* Pamphlet I, p. 17.
[86] *Ibid.,* p. 18. [87] *Ibid.*

of any proponents of the presidential form. Perhaps for the same reason Israelis were not as disturbed by the evils of the multiple party system as Americans would be. The General Zionists, who were disturbed, constitute the party with the strongest British and American influences. Yet it is also possible that the comparatively negligible amount of attention given the problem by the theorists and spokesmen of the various parties indicates that they either despaired of changing the situation or were more interested in their own parties' survival than with the over-all welfare of the state.

What is also significant is that the parties seem to take it for granted that the extension of government action will not lead to the decline of freedom. The spokesmen of the labor parties seem to have had no fears that personal freedom in Israel would be in jeopardy even if the State or the Histadrut held a monopoly over all phases of the economy. Moreover, the religious parties gave assurances that they would never interfere with anyone's freedom of conscience, but thus far they have failed to publish even one article proving that this concession is supported by Jewish law.

The preoccupation of all the parties with the status quo and their myopic concern with one issue—how to assure their own success—reduce the value of the literature on the constitution. Even the religious parties did not seek to deduce from biblical and talmudic materials what the ideal state should be. No new insight on political institutions or human rights was forthcoming. Nor did the labor parties adduce one recommendation which was born of the unique character of Israeli's cooperative or collectivist settlements. Mapam's recommendations also reflected only its desire to protect its own status as an opposition party and little more. Perhaps in the future Israel's political literature will be written by persons who are not professional party politicians, and then it will command more universal interest.

CHAPTER III

The Parties' Official Statements on the Constitution

The political parties officially presented their views at sessions of a special committee of the State Council of the Provisional Government. These views have already played an important part in the shaping of constitutional patterns and will undoubtedly influence later developments. Dr. Leo Kohn, whose draft of a constitution was fully debated by this committee, was an influential employee of the Government, in its Foreign Ministry, during the period of the First Kneset. The members of the committee themselves were members of the First Kneset. Five of them were members of the First Kneset's Committee on the Constitution, Law, and Justice;[1] one of them was chairman of that committee. However, despite the importance of the views expressed and the conclusions reached, the party spokesmen still ignored the problem of personal freedom in a planned economy and even the religionists made only insignificant recommendations specifically derived from the Torah.

DRAFTS OF KOHN AND VITTA

The Committee on the Constitution was nominated by the Committee on Committees of the State Council of the Provisional Government.[2] The committee was to consist of eight members, but Mapai, which was entitled to two of the eight, designated only

[1] A. Zidon, *ha-Kneset* (Tel Aviv, 5710), pp. 108-9.
[2] *M.H.H. Proceedings*, ninth meeting, p. 12.

one.[3] The State Council elected the seven members[4] who did serve, and they met some twenty-three times.[5] The summaries of their deliberations were subsequently edited by their chairman and published by the State Council.[6]

Though three other drafts of a constitution were submitted to the State Council,[7] the committee decided to use Kohn's[8] as the basis for discussion; it was to his draft that the committee's "general debate" on the subject was directed during its first three meetings on August 11, August 18, and September 8, 1948.[9] Professor Asher Vitta, special adviser to the committee, also prepared an almost complete draft which was considered later in connection with the debate on the legislative and executive authorities.[10]

Dr. Kohn's draft consisted of a preamble and nine chapters. The first chapter dealt with general principles, such as the name of the state (sec. 1), its democratic character (sec. 2), its official languages (sec. 5), its flag (sec. 7), citizenship (sec. 6), and the right of all Jews to immigrate (sec. 3). The second chapter dealt with human rights and fundamental freedoms. The legislative and the executive authorities were described in the third and fourth chapters, respectively. They provided for a parliamentary form of government, with the popular election of a Chamber of Deputies (sec. 27) by proportional representation (sec. 29).

[3] *Ibid.* [4] *Ibid.* [5] Zidon, *ha-Kneset*, p. 29.

[6] These are herein cited as *Wa'adat ha-Huqah Proceedings*. The chairman of the committee was Zorah Wahrhaftig of ha-Po'el ha-Mizrahi. Meir Grabovsky represented Mapai; Yizhar Harari the General Zionists; Barukh Weinstein the Revisionists; Meir David Loewenstein the Agudat Yisrael; Schmuel Mikunis the Communists; and Zevi Luria, Mapam. Harari later joined the Progressive Party. Meir Vilner was Mikunis's alternate. Nahum Nir-Raffalkes replaced Luria after the twelfth committee meeting. See *W.H. Proceedings*, Pamphlet IV, p. 3.

[7] *Shenaton ha-Memshalah, 5710*, p. 6.

[8] Dr. Kohn's draft, with his commentary, was published as Pamphlet II of the *W.H. Proceedings*.

[9] *W.H. Proceedings*, Pamphlet I, pp. 1, 3.

[10] Professor Vitta's recommendations to the committee were published as Pamphlet V of the *W.H. Proceedings*.

Representation was not to be national, however, but rather from an unspecified number of election zones *(ibid.).* The president was to have very limited powers, while a Ministers' Council or cabinet would exercise the executive authority and be responsible to the legislature (sec. 64). An auditor and comptroller who was not a member of the legislature would supervise all accounts (sec. 69). The judicial authority was described in the fifth chapter. It would be exercised by a series of courts culminating in a Supreme Court. A separate system of religious courts would continue to function in limited areas (sec. 70). The sixth chapter dealt with the amending process (sec. 75); the seventh chapter provided for judicial review of the constitutionality of laws (sec. 76); the eighth chapter "received" the existing system of law with several limitations (sec. 77); the ninth chapter dealt with promulgation.

Professor Vitta's draft also consisted of nine chapters. The first dealt with the legislature; the second with the presidency; the third with the Government; the fourth with a projected State Council, and the fifth with a Council of the Comptroller. The next three chapters described three types of courts: civil, ecclesiastical, and constitutional. The ninth chapter dealt with the amending process. Vitta's differences with Kohn will be discussed in connection with the different organs of the state to which they refer.

VIEWS OF THE SECULARIST PARTIES

While each member of the committee articulated his party's views regarding the general nature of the constitution,[11] the general debate added a number of specific recommendations.

Barukh Weinstein—the Revisionist—stressed the fact that the constitution must take into account the destiny of Jews who live beyond the territorial limits. "Our state was not established as an entity without ties to multitudes scattered everywhere."[12] He therefore suggested that citizenship be granted not only to those

[11] See *supra,* Chapter II. [12] *W.H. Proceedings,* Pamphlet I, p. 6.

Jews who have already emigrated to Israel but also to those who are without any other citizenship, even when they are stateless as a matter of choice.

Mapai's spokesman, Meir Grabovsky, differed with him. He opposed the granting of citizenship to persons outside of Israel. He did, however, say that no time limit should be set for the privilege of a Jew to emigrate to Israel and that a Jew who comes to Israel should be eligible for citizenship within six months after his arrival, though a longer waiting period might be provided for others.[13]

Was the difference in point of view based on party ideologies or programs?

Mapai's principal source of strength in the World Zionist movement has always been within Israel, while the other parties derive their principal support from without Israel. One may charge that that accounts for Mapai's reluctance to see too many grants of citizenship outside the state. Yet the difference in point of view may derive from the fact that the Revisionists' suggestion was simply bold and unprecedented—at least before the days of fascism—and as such would be frowned upon by most constitution planners committed to the more generally accepted political theories. As a matter of fact it was Grabovsky who, on behalf of Mapai, gave evidence of conservative proclivities, and he expressed the greatest misgivings about radical democratic techniques.[14]

He said that with their blood the people acquire control of their government only to see it degenerate so that even a barbarous Hitler can become their master. Parliamentary crises, such as France and Italy are wont to have, are conducive to the usurpation of power by the executive, and then dictatorship follows. He would, therefore, favor any scheme that would do justice to democratic ideals and yet eliminate the threat of such crises.

His misgivings about democracy caused him to urge even the

[13] *Ibid.*, p. 8.

[14] *Ibid.*, p. 7.

curbing of freedom of expression: an unbridled press—even the unbridled use of placards—is hardly conducive to the best political education of the masses.[15] To the use of the referendum he was violently opposed. He said that elections in Israel should be infrequent and that statutes should provide for limitation of campaign expenses. He further asserted that the tensions caused by elections are such that considerable time is needed thereafter to create a smoothly functioning administration, and the immigrants' political backgrounds are so heterogeneous that frequent elections and referenda would only cause them to retain party loyalties acquired elsewhere instead of becoming assimilated politically into existing party frameworks.

Grabovsky's opposition to the referendum was particularly interesting because the Revisionists—the rightists in economic thought—favored it.[16] They favored it as a check on the unicameral legislature. They also favored the direct election of the president by popular vote and constitutional amendments by the people.[17] Furthermore, they felt that civil servants and members of the regular army should not be eligible for election to the lawmaking body.[18]

One may wonder why such democratic proposals were favored by a rightist party. Yet what the Revisionists most desired was to break what they regard as Mapai's stranglehold on the legislature, the executive, the army, and the civil service. Their democratic proposals, if adopted, might help to fulfill this aim. That is also why they favored the severance of all party ties by the president and speaker of the legislature after their election,[19] to which Mapai objected.[20] Thus one beholds again evidence of the parties' preoccupation with the immediate improvement of their own position rather than concern for the ultimate fulfillment of either their conservative or liberal, capitalist or socialist philosophies.

Weinstein also criticized Kohn's draft of a constitution for its

[15] *Ibid.*, p. 8.
[16] *Ibid.*, p. 7.
[17] *Ibid.*, p. 6.
[18] *Ibid.*
[19] *Ibid.*
[20] *Ibid.*, p. 9.

support of cooperative economic enterprise while remaining silent on private enterprise;[21] thus ignoring the fact that the development of the country's resources will require extensive capital, and for that reason investors should be encouraged to come to the land. Mapai's spokesman raised no such objection to Kohn's draft,[22] but Mapam's spokesman felt that it did not go far enough in its support of socialism:[23] the right to work should not only be mentioned in the constitution but the Government should be made responsible for its implementation. By the same token the right to an education should not only be mentioned in the constitution but the Government should be ordered to provide free schools for everyone. In addition he suggested that the state be required to develop the resources of the land.[24] And the preference for cooperative enterprise should apply to industry and commerce as well as to agriculture. Such a clause need not exclude private enterprise; however, the nationalization of the land, water, electricity, minerals, and oil, should be mentioned as the ultimate goal.[25]

The Communist party spokesman agreed, saying that while he knew that it was impractical now to propose a socialist constitution, he did feel that it was important to include social and economic rights therein and to provide for their implementation. Furthermore, to guarantee civil and political equality would mean nothing unless all citizens were to have equal access to the resources necessary to conduct political campaigns.[26] "The equal right of every citizen to sleep under a bridge" is not equality. Therefore the constitution must oblige the Government to make meeting halls, printing presses, and broadcasting stations equally available for political work by all groups without cost.

[21] *Ibid.*, p. 6.

[22] Dr. Kohn's draft had Mapai's general approval. See Karl I. Friedrich, " 'Al Huqat Medinat Yisrael" (On the Constitution of the State of Israel), *Molad*, II, No. 10 (Tevet, 5709: January, 1949), 203-7.

[23] *W.H. Proceedings*, Pamphlet I, p. 15.

[24] *Ibid.*, p. 16. [25] *Ibid.* [26] *Ibid.*, p. 17.

The spokesmen for Mapam and the Communists were also critical of Kohn's failure to provide adequately for the rights of Arabs. While they did not demand the actual creation of a binational state, they maintained that the constitution should not evade realities. Simply to mention minorities, as if the Arab minority was no more significant than a handful of Russians living in Jerusalem, was deemed neither fair nor practical.[27] Furthermore, to attempt to create a uninational state would be inconsistent with the United Nations plan that the whole of Palestine remain one unit with at least an economic union of Arab and Jewish states. If Arabs were to enjoy full equality in Israel there would be peace without as well as within, and the whole of the land would remain a unit.[28] If Arabic were to be a second language for all of Israel and not only an official language in areas where Arabs reside, the Arabs would be assured political and cultural equality.[29]

The same two spokesmen criticized the religious tone of Kohn's draft, while Mapai's spokesman was silent on the religious issue. This silence was virtually the offer of an olive branch to the religious parties with which Mapai formed a coalition in the period of the First Kneset. Certainly it did not reflect the antireligious views of many, or most, of Mapai's members. Again considerations of party advantage rather than long-range constitution planning came to the fore.

Zevi Luria, representing Mapam, objected that the preamble to Dr. Kohn's draft had such a religious tone that only a professing Jew could ever take an oath to support the constitution and thus hold office.[30] He contended that freedom of conscience had to be assured not only to Christians and Muslims but also to Jews, and that there should be civil marriage for those who did not want any religious solemnization whatever—this to include non-Jews as well. However, he saw no objection to the ordaining of the religious festivals as national holidays, nor any objection to

[27] *Ibid.*, p. 16. [28] *Ibid.*, p. 15. [29] *Ibid.* [30] *Ibid.*, p. 14.

special privileges for Jews with regard to immigration to Israel, for Mapam was committed to the philosophy and program of Zionism—not only Communism.

The Communist party spokesman, on the other hand, objected particularly to the provision that the president must be a Jew,[31] and he also felt that the granting of special privileges to Jews outside of Israel should be limited to emergencies where there is danger to life and limb. He did not mention the danger of cultural extinction which many Israeli Jews fear will come to pass upon their brethren in countries behind the "Iron Curtain."

The spokesman for the General Zionists, Yizhar Harari, did express middle-of-the-road points of view. He objected to slavish compliance with all the provisions of the United Nations General Assembly resolution as urged by the "left." The "left" apparently felt that what once had the approval of the USSR was unalterable. That resolution sought to protect the Arab minority, but, Harari argued, if to this end the constitution were to incorporate all of its provisions, the result might be the creation of a binational state and numerous other anomalies. Arabs should enjoy complete equality but not special privileges because they are Arabs.[32] As an example he cited the clause providing that no land belonging to Arabs shall be taken even for a public purpose without compensation. How would this affect the prevailing rule that 25 percent of a man's land can be confiscated without compensation if the purpose is the widening of highways? Would Arabs be exempt from this rule? Furthermore, should the Government be compelled, as required by the resolution, to publish an Arabic newspaper, and not be compelled to publish a Hebrew one? By the same token the constitution should not disqualify an Arab from becoming president of the state. Even if rights are given to ethnic groups for some modicum of autonomy, no one ethnic group should be mentioned by name.

Harari continued by saying that the constitution should give

[31] *Ibid.*, p. 18.

[32] *Ibid.*, p. 10.

some recognition to the ties that bind Jews everywhere to the land; at least the right of immigration had to be assured.[33] And, in addition, if the legislature is bicameral, the president of the World Zionist Organization might be a member of the upper house. Grabovsky asked him how this suggestion could be reconciled with a clause guaranteeing full and equal privileges even to Arabs.[34] Harari replied that anyone could become president of the World Zionist movement.

Harari also suggested that citizenship be granted to Jews outside of Israel who rendered services to the country, particularly to Jews in distress who could be helped by such a privilege. And lastly, he suggested a specific provision that an unconstitutional law be a nullity.[35] Again one beholds western influence principally on the views of the General Zionists.

VIEWS OF THE RELIGIOUS PARTIES

While the "left" criticized Dr. Kohn's draft because it was too religious in character, the religious parties criticized it because it was too elusive on the question of religion. Zorah Wahrhaftig, representing Mizrahi and ha-Po'el ha-Mizrahi, pointed out that Zionist Congresses in the past always affirmed the view that nothing would ever be done by the Zionist Organization that would be inconsistent with Judaism; the least that the constitution had now to assure was that the state would do nothing thus inconsistent.[36]

Furthermore, the right of religious communities to organize and enjoy the protection of the law, as well as tax exemptions, should come within the scope of the constitution. These communities should also be subsidized by the state.[37]

Some orthodox Jews, he added,[38] take the view that if the state becomes secular in character they would "ghettoize" themselves, establish their own courts and seek from the state only the privilege of being tried in such courts. Another group, however, would

[33] *Ibid.*, p. 13. [34] *Ibid.* [35] *Ibid.*
[36] *Ibid.*, p. 19. [37] *Ibid.* [38] *Ibid.*, p. 21.

rather see a unified nation and the assimilation by the prevailing law of the traditional concepts or rules of Jewish law. Such an approach would contribute to the ultimate unity of the legal system as well as the unity of the people.

The state, he argued, ought to have an unmistakably Jewish character. The Jews were given only a part of the land to establish their own state—even as the Arabs were given a part. Of course, the rights of Arabs must be guaranteed, but Hebrew in the Jewish state should be the only official language and the president ineligible unless he is a Jew.[39]

Wahrhaftig did suggest at least one way in which traditional Jewish law might be used as the basis for a distinction between alienable and inalienable land. However, he too failed to draw upon Jewish law for recommendations with respect to the executive and legislative authorities, their constitution, their power, their limitations. Is there a dearth of such materials or is there rather a reluctance on the part of the religious parties to be specific?

Meir David Loewenstein, representing Agudat Yisrael, said that from the point of view of his party there need be no constitution at all. The Torah includes not only doctrines for man's spiritual guidance but also directives for every phase of man's individual and social existence. Therefore it should be adequate to say "Israel's Torah is her constitution."[40] But he was no more enlightening than Wahrhaftig.

"Alas," said he, "our generation is not equal to such a lofty view!" Yet all the drafts were objectionable to him, for in all the "Torah is separated from the state"[41]—made a matter of individual conscience. He suggested, therefore, that among the general principles there be included a statement to the effect that the Torah is Israel's constitution, but all non-Jewish religious communities shall enjoy full freedom in matters of conscience.

What did this "freedom" mean? Did it mean that they could

[39] *Ibid.* [40] *Ibid.*, p. 22. [41] *Ibid.*

also engage in missionary activity? And what freedom of conscience would Jews enjoy? To what extent did the Torah permit such freedom and to what extent was coercion required? Loewenstein gave no answer.

He did want a prohibition against the conscription of women[42] and the substitution of the word "declare" for the word "swear" in oaths.[43]

After the general debate the committee prepared drafts of two important articles of the constitution—one on the legislative authority[44] and the other on the executive authority.[45] These became the basis for the Transition Law approved by the First Kneset. However, these important articles did not involve to any great extent the fundamental differences in ideology which the "general debate" revealed. The "general debate" was rather one of the previews of the debate to be held in the Kneset in 1950 on the need for a written constitution.[46] It gave further evidence, however, of the inability of the constitution's framers to soar above immediate party problems and project themselves over the future, its requirements and its possibilities. Not a word was said about divesting party leaders of their control over the parties and nominations, nor was one recommendation offered to give the people a sense of personal contact with their government.

EVALUATION

Why was there almost no reference whatever in the debate to the political theory of Judaism or at least to political ideas contained in the literature of Judaism? The Bible did not serve the party spokesmen even as much as it did the political philosophers of the Middle Ages or the Reformation. And the considerable juridic materials of the sea of the Talmud, which at least the re-

[42] *Ibid.*, p. 23.

[43] *Ibid.* The word presently used is "Mit-hayyev" (to pledge or obligate one's self). *Divrei ha-Kneset*, I, 1st Sess. first meeting, 8.

[44] *W.H. Proceedings*, Pamphlet III, pp. 66-70.

[45] *Ibid.*, Pamphlet IV, pp. 38-45.

[46] See *infra*, Chapter VIII.

ligionists might have used, were never even mentioned. Many reasons can be given.

First, there is no definitive political philosophy in Judaism, any more than there is a definitive political philosophy in other religions. Both secularists and religionists could have used biblical and talmudic materials to sustain their point of view.

Second, the rabbinical seminaries of Palestine and Israel taught and developed talmudic learning for centuries with such oblivion of western categories of thought that the terminology of sovereignty, authority, power, constitutional limitations, and mixed government was never related to the source materials of Judaism.

Third, when in very recent years there was a decided trend in the direction of applying talmudic sources to the theoretical foundations and practical institutions of a modern state, the emphasis was on civil and criminal jurisprudence rather than on public law.

Thus, for example, when Dr. Leo Kohn provided in his draft constitution for the judicial review of legislation, he indicated that the notion was inspired by American practice, and even he—one of the religionists in Israel—did not refer to the much older talmudic source. The Jewish equivalent of judicial review was simply not recognized.[47] Kohn, however, was aware of the talmudic point of view on capital punishment. That was private, not public, law.

Fourth, none of the party spokesmen was concerned with the preparation of a really new constitution. All of them assumed that the system within the Kneset Israel would continue with some modifications. The religious parties, therefore, sought only to make some further gains with respect to the inclusion of more of Jewish law into the legal order. Not one was prepared to challenge foundations, and even Agudat Yisrael was not prepared to state whether the Torah would have called for a presidential form

[47] See E. Rackman, "Talmudic Insights on Human Rights," *Judaism*, I, No. 2 (April, 1952), 158-59.

of government instead of a parliamentary one, or whether the time had in fact come to plan for the reestablishment of monarchy.

Because the debate yielded so little that was new from the point of view of either the secularists or the religionists, it was disappointing. Perhaps a constitutional convention after a decade or more of independence will be more fruitful.

CHAPTER IV

Contributions of the Provisional Government to Constitutional Development

THE PROVISIONAL GOVERNMENT

Ten days before the new State was born, the Mo'ezet ha-'Am (People's Council) convened in Tel Aviv. During its last two meetings on May 14 it drafted the Proclamation of Independence, promulgated it, and declared itself to be the Provisional State Council—the legislative authority of Israel.[1] The Provisional Government would be its executive arm, with power to enact emergency legislation.[2]

The portfolios in the Provisional Government were distributed among the parties as follows:[3]

- Four to Mapai
  - Head of the Government and Defense
  - Finance
  - Transport and Communications
  - Foreign Affairs
- Two to Mapam
  - Labor and Development
  - Agriculture
- Three to the General Zionists
  - Trade, Industry, and Supply

[1] *Mo'ezet ha-'Am Proceedings* (Tel Aviv, 1948), pp. 24-25.
[2] *Ibid.*, p. 26. [3] *Shenaton ha-Memshalah, 5710*, p. 4.

Interior
Justice
One to Mizrahi
Religions and Veterans' Welfare
One to ha-Po'el ha-Mizrahi
Immigration and Health
One to Agudat Yisrael
Welfare
One to the Sephardim
Police and Minorities

The ministers so organized their departments that very few changes were made even after the Constituent Assembly convened. These are fully described in the Government Yearbooks.[4] The ministers' immediate and continuing preoccupation with legislation was noteworthy. They drafted all the Pequdot (decrees or ordinances) and budgets, which were submitted to the Provisional Government as a whole for approval. The decree would be prepared, after consultation with the Ministry of Justice, by the department ultimately responsible for its execution. After the Government as a whole had given its approval, the decree was submitted directly to that committee of the State Council which was concerned with its subject matter as well as to the State Council's committee on legislation. The latter committee was to examine the proposal only from a formal, juridic point of view, but it often exceeded its mandate and considered the substance of the legislation as well. After due consideration by the two committees, the proposed decree was explained in the State Council, usually by the minister concerned, and read aloud by one of the secretaries. The chairman of the committee that considered the substance of the decree sometimes added comments. Following this there was a general debate together with the offering of

[4] The Government Yearbooks for 5711 and 5712 were translated into English. See *infra*, p. 105.

amendments by members of the State Council who, in either of the committees that considered the decree, had reserved their right to do so.

The proposed decree was then voted upon, paragraph by paragraph, with the vote on proposed amendments taken first. Thereafter there was a vote on the decree as a whole.[5]

Members of the State Council directed written questions to the ministers for reply at a stated session. They also received full reports from the ministers on important problems—the war, foreign affairs, immigration, and development—which reports they debated freely. Those procedures, however, were not new. They had prevailed in the Asefat ha-Nivharim of the Kneset Israel.

On May 14, 1948, the State Council "received" the then prevailing system of law, except as thereafter changed or as necessarily modified by the very fact that a new state existed.[6]

On May 16, the State Council elected Chaim Weizmann to the presidency of the State. The Proclamation of Independence did not provide for such an office. David Ben Gurion, however, pleaded during the first meeting of the State Council that its members rise above juridic considerations and pay this much deserved tribute to Professor Weizmann. Nonetheless, he stated that Weizmann would not be a member of the Provisional Government.[7] In fact, the President had no powers whatever until the Constituent Assembly convened and the Transition Law was approved. His office had no constitutional basis and no budgetary allocation.[8]

Three days later the State Council declared a state of emer-

[5] A. Zidon, *ha-Kneset* (Tel Aviv, 5710), pp. 23-24. See also *infra*, pp. 55-56 on procedure in the State Council.

[6] *Mo'ezet ha-'Am Proceedings*, p. 26.

[7] *M.H.H. Proceedings*, first meeting, p. 7.

[8] *Shenaton ha-Memshalah, 5710*, p. 45. It is also reported that the president was subjected to a number of restrictions in his official life. See K. Bilby, *New Star in the Near East* (New York, 1951), p. 166. It would appear from the text that Bilby referred to the period of the Provisional Government.

gency[9] and approved a more specific decree with regard to both government and law,[10] which became known as the Law and Administrative Ordinance. The personnel of the Council was given by names, as well as the personnel of the Government. Parties were not mentioned.[11] Authority was reserved to the Council to enlarge its membership and that of the Government by the addition of Arab representatives. The Government was to fix the boundaries of districts, while municipal administrations were to continue functioning as theretofore.

The Council was to approve budgets, the levying of taxes, and the incurring of indebtedness. The ministers of the Government, however, could issue administrative regulations to implement any law approved by the Council. If the Council proclaimed a state of emergency, the Government could issue executive orders called for by the emergency. These orders might even modify or nullify a law approved by the Council. In such a case, however, the orders would be valid for only three months, unless they were sooner repealed or their validity was extended by the Council. If the Council declared the emergency to have ended, the executive orders predicated on the emergency were repealed.[12]

All decrees became effective with their publication in the

[9] *'Iton Rishmi,* No. 2, May 21, 1948, p. 6.

[10] The full text is in the *M.H.H. Proceedings,* second meeting, pp. 15-19, and in *'Iton Rishmi,* No. 2, Supp., May 21, 1948, pp. 1-5.

[11] Parties were not mentioned even in the amendment to the Law and Administration Ordinance which provided for the manner in which vacancies in the State Council would be filled (*ibid.,* No. 4, June 9, 1948, p. 16). The State Council filled such vacancies, but in practice nominees of the political parties whose representatives resigned or could not function were elected by the Council. The same applied to alternates for any meeting of the Council (*M.H.H. Proceedings,* third meeting, pp. 4-5).

[12] Section 9 of the Law and Administration Ordinance reads as follows:

(a) If the Provisional State Council should deem it expedient, it may declare that a state of emergency exists in the State, and upon such declaration being published in the Official Gazette, the Provisional Government may authorize the Head of the Government or any minister to make such

'Iton Rishmi (Official Gazette), unless another effective date was specified (sec. 10).

All privileges of the King of England and his officials, as well as all privileges theretofore enjoyed by British citizens, were terminated (sec. 12). All functions theretofore performed by the mandatory were to be performed by the Council and Government (sec. 14). All Jews who had theretofore immigrated illegally were to be deemed legal immigrants as of the date of their arrival (sec. 13). All directives in any statute or regulation requiring the use of the English language were also repealed. Other laws, which were "received" by the new State, and which required some amendment because of the new political situation, could be promulgated by the Minister of Justice and published in the *'Iton Rishmi.* Taxes theretofore paid to the mandatory would now be payable to the new State. The existing court system was also retained. Property rights were not altered, whether or not they were vested in individuals or corporations. The regulations, however, of the Wa'ad Leumi, which were promulgated after November 29, 1947, the date of the United Nations General Assembly resolution, were given the status of law (sec. 19).

On June 3 those civil servants and police who worked for the mandatory were transferred to the appropriate departments of the new State. Yet, the Provisional Government could, in its

---

emergency regulations as he may deem expedient in the interest of the defense of the State, military security and the maintenance of supplies and essential services.

(b) An emergency regulation may alter any law, temporarily suspend it, or condition it, and may also impose or increase taxes or other obligatory payments.

(c) An emergency regulation shall expire three months after it is made, unless it is extended or revoked sooner by a decree of the Provisional State Council, or revoked by the authority that made it.

(d) When the Provisional State Council shall deem it proper, it may proclaim that the state of emergency has ended and when this will have been proclaimed in the *Official Gazette,* the emergency regulations will expire on the dates fixed in the proclamation.

These provisions were not repealed by the First Kneset.

absolute discretion, within six months,[13] terminate their employment or transfer them.

However, it was June 17 before the Council considered and established its own rules of procedure,[14] which became the pattern for the Constituent Assembly and the First Kneset. It revealed the extent to which the Government would control the legislature. The Government was to prepare the agenda to which additions could be made by members of the State Council. The Government's items, however, enjoyed priority (sec. 4). The legislators' right of debate was well guarded, and every party was virtually guaranteed an opportunity to be heard on all important measures (sec. 5). A Government spokesman, however, would have the right to speak at any time (sec. 8).

A member of the Council, desirous of proposing legislation, first had to submit the bill to the minister who might be responsible for its execution, if passed, and to the parliamentary committee concerned with that ministry. If the committee defeated it, he could not bring it to the Council unless he had forthwith reserved that right. However, he had the privilege of being heard before the committee, even if he were not a member of it (secs. 8, 11, and 12). Most bills, however, were brought by a minister of the Government directly to the appropriate committee of the Council. There was usually one debate in the Council covering all matters general and specific, with a vote taken immediately thereafter.

Questions directed to the executive had to be submitted forty-eight hours before the session of the Council, and the executive authority might reply orally or in writing (secs. 13 and 14). However, only the opening half-hour of each session was devoted to replies by ministers. No quorum was specified for the opening of a session or for a vote.

[13] *'Iton Rishmi*, No. 4, Supp. 1, June 9, 1948, pp. 12-13. This was later extended for another 4 months (December 9, 1948) (*ibid.*, No. 36, Supp. 1, p. 72).

[14] *M.H.H. Proceedings*, fourth meeting, pp. 46-48.

The executive might call for a roll-call vote, or any ten members of the Council (approximately 27 percent) might demand it. The same rule applied to a secret written ballot. Otherwise voting was by the raising of hands. A majority of those voting was necessary for the success of a measure (secs. 17 and 18).

On June 24, 1948, the decree establishing the Supreme Court was approved by the Council.[15] Again the power of the Government was extended. The Minister of Justice was to nominate the judges, who were to be appointed by the Government with the Council's ratification. The Minister of Justice also fixed rules of procedure and fulfilled all the regulative functions performed under the mandatory by the presiding judge of the Supreme Court (sec. 10).

On July 1 the Council determined how the parties were to be represented in the various committees, and on July 8 the appointments were made.[16] Persons who were not members thereof were eligible for appointment as consultants. The eleven committees established were the Committee on Committees, the Committee on the Constitution, the Committee to Prepare for the Election of Representatives to the Constituent Assembly, the Committee on Finance and Economy, the Committee on Legislation, the Committee on Security, the Committee on Foreign Affairs, the Committee on Immigration, the Committee on Interior, the Committee on Public Services, and the Committee on Flag and Symbol.

DECREE FOR ELECTIONS TO CONSTITUENT ASSEMBLY

The debate in the State Council preliminary to the passage of the decree dealing with the election of delegates to the Constituent Assembly was a prolonged one, and the Pequdat ha-

[15] *'Iton Rishmi,* No. 7, Supp. 1, June 30, 1948, pp. 17-18.

[16] Each committee consisted of two members drawn from Mapai, and one from each of the following parties: Mapam, General Zionists, Mizrahi and ha-Po'el ha-Mizrahi, Revisionists, and usually one or more representatives of the smaller parties.

Behirot l'Asefah ha-Mekhonenet (Decree for Elections to the Constituent Assembly)[17] was quite involved. Its importance, however, cannot be gainsaid.

The special committee[18] to draft the decree had met some ten times before the State Council[19] began its consideration of the proposed ordinance on October 28, 1948.[20] The Council itself was concerned with the elections and the projected Constituent Assembly until its very last session on February 10, 1949. The issues debated have great constitutional significance, though the electoral system that was established was very similar to the one prevailing in the Kneset Israel.[21]

The committee itself denied that its proposed decree would have lasting significance. For example, many of its members felt that the ultimate constitution should provide for district representation in any legislative body to be created. They did not believe that the pattern of nationwide representation should be used for any election other than the one for the Constituent Assembly. For the Constituent Assembly, however, each party could provide a slate for all seats. So established is this pattern that no change whatever has as yet been made.

The committee did recommend that, although voting for a party list, voters should have the right to strike out names on the list and substitute others. This recommendation was defeated,[22] though there could be deletions and substitutions in the elections for the Asefat ha-Nivharim of the Kneset Israel.[23]

[17] *'Iton Rishmi,* No. 33, Supp. 1, November 19, 1948, pp. 52-60.

[18] This committee consisted of two representatives of Mapai and one of each of the remaining parties represented in the State Council. They could cast as many votes, however, as their party had seats in the Council (Zidon, *ha-Kneset,* p. 37).

[19] *M.H.H. Proceedings,* twenty-fourth meeting, p. 16.

[20] *Ibid.*

[21] See *Official Gazette of the Government of Palestine,* No. 254, March 1, 1930, pp. 142-45.

[22] *M.H.H. Proceedings,* twenty-sixth meeting, p. 26.

[23] Paragraphs 15 and 21 of the Regulations, *Official Gazette of the Government of Palestine,* March 1, 1930, pp. 143-44.

Thus the elections became national and for party slates, and the control of the parties' leaders over elections was extended.

The decree itself consisted of eight chapters. The first set forth the general principle of a national, secret, and direct election with proportional representation (sec. 3). The number of persons to be elected would be 120 (sec. 8). The second chapter described the organization of the central election board with party representation thereon proportional to the party representation in the State Council (sec. 11*b*), the powers of said board (sec. 12), and its appointment of local boards of election (sec. 13). The preparation of electors' lists was described in the third chapter and the submission of lists of candidates in the fourth chapter. By section 26 any two parties were permitted to effect an agreement with each other with regard to the division of surplus votes. The fifth chapter described the place and time of voting (sec. 27), identification cards (sec. 28), and the manner of voting (sec. 29).

Chapter six stipulated the manner of apportioning the votes. The total number of valid votes cast was to be divided by 121 to yield the "general quotient." The number of votes cast for a party list was to be divided by the quotient to obtain the number of representatives each party had elected (sec. 30, *a* and *b*). The remaining seats were divided as follows (sec. 30*c*): Each party which had elected at least one candidate was assigned a "list quotient." The "list quotient" was computed by dividing the total number of votes cast for the party list by the number of representatives elected from that list, plus one. The party list with the largest such "list quotient" elected another representative, then the second largest, the third largest, and so forth, until all the remaining seats were assigned. If there was still a remainder, the procedure was followed again, with the addition, however, of one to the divisor to arrive at the new "list quotient."

For the purpose of section 30*c*, parties could agree in advance to merge their votes (sec. 31). The order of the candidates on the list would be the order in which they were elected (sec. 32*a*), and if any representative resigned, died, or was disqualified, he would be succeeded by the next available person in his list (sec. 32). The rest of the chapter dealt with the manner of counting the votes, reporting, and publicizing the results, as well as challenges to the results.

Chapters seven and eight established penalties for interference with the elections (sec. 37) and for illegal voting (sec. 40), and provided for deferred elections in an area where the war prevented voting from taking place (sec. 44).

On one issue—the proposed granting of rights to non-Israeli Jews—the committee that prepared the decree found itself in utter disagreement with the Provisional Government. The committee had recommended that Jews in Cyprus have the right to vote in the forthcoming elections. They argued that these Jews were in fact citizens whom the British had deported. In the Council it was suggested that the right be given also to Jews still in displaced persons assembly centers in Europe, for they too, as prospective immigrants, should have a voice in the Constituent Assembly. The Government, on the other hand, argued that all of these proposals were impractical. How could such elections be supervised? How could any Israeli court exercise jurisdiction over disputes arising with regard to an election in such places? The Government's argument went still further. It warned that if Jews outside of Israel were given the right of franchise, then the same privilege must be accorded refugee Arabs in the Muslim countries to which they had fled. Otherwise, world public opinion might justly complain that the Jews were discriminating against Arabs.

The Government's view prevailed, but so heated was the debate that the Head of the Government himself felt impelled to participate and to add to the effectiveness of the presentation of the Minister of the Interior.[24]

[24] *M.H.H. Proceedings*, twenty-sixth meeting, pp. 8-10.

Regarding the number of seats in the Constituent Assembly, the Council was fairly well divided. The smaller parties wanted 171 seats, thereby insuring a larger number of their own delegates. This was also the number in the Asefat ha-Nivharim of the Kneset Israel. The committee had recommended 101, though even 71 and 85 were suggested. The majority of the Council favored 120 (sec. 8). The reason is interesting. Dr. Wahrhaftig had proposed 120 because he felt that constitutional patterns should, as far as possible, have roots in the Jewish tradition. When the Jews returned to Palestine after the Babylonian Captivity of 586 B.C.E. they were governed by the Men of the Great Synagogue, who numbered 120.[25] Dr. Wahrhaftig had also urged,[26] again relying on tradition, that candidates should be twenty years of age before they were regarded as eligible for election. The committee and the Council preferred twenty-one as the age for candidates (sec. 5).[27] Voters, however, need be only eighteen years of age (sec. 4).[28]

The right of civil servants to be candidates also evoked considerable attention. There were many suggestions, but the committee's original recommendation was approved. Civil servants were required to take leave of their offices as soon as their candidacy was fully confirmed. They could return to their positions after the elections, if they were defeated. If they were successful, their leaves would be extended until after the conclusion of the sessions of the Constituent Assembly (sec. 7).[29]

The Government, however, was less concerned with this problem than it was with the problem of the chairmanship of the Board of Elections. This Board was to consist of 19 members, representative of all the parties in the Council (sec. 10*b*). How-

[25] *Ibid.*, twenty-fifth meeting, p. 20.

[26] *Ibid.*, p. 16. [27] *Ibid.*, p. 17.

[28] Under the electoral law for the Kneset Israel the eligibility age of voters was twenty, and of candidates twenty-five (paragraphs 6 and 7 of the Regulations, *Official Gazette of the Government of Palestine*, March 1, 1930, p. 142).

[29] *'Iton Rishmi*, No. 33, Supp. 1, November 19, 1948, p. 52.

ever, the Government wanted a justice of the Supreme Court to be its chairman.[30] The committee insisted that the Board elect its own chairman. The Council again upheld the Government. The Council, however, did not approve of a proposal that every district board of elections have as its presiding officer a district court judge.[31]

The party representation in the Board of Elections was as follows: Mapai, 4; Mapam, 2; Mizrahi and ha-Po'el ha-Mizrahi, 2; Progressives, 2; Revisionists, 2; Agudat Yisrael, 1; WIZO, 1; Po'alei Agudat Yisrael, 1; and Sephardim, 1.[32]

The Council also discussed the use of the judiciary to resolve issues that might be raised regarding the legality of any candidate's election. The committee had recommended—and its recommendation was approved—that the Constituent Assembly itself determine the legality of election results (sec. 35).[33] Wahrhaftig had proposed that such issues be resolved by the courts. Opposition to his view was predicated on two grounds: first, the "law's delays" might delay the work of the Constituent Assembly; second, when elected, the Constituent Assembly would be the sovereign organ of the nation, whose powers the State Council could not restrict.[34]

One recommendation of the committee, however, was rejected. It is of interest because it reveals how serious was the problem created by the terrorists. The committee recommended that election to the Constituent Assembly automatically release an imprisoned candidate from his confinement. A Mapai spokesman prevailed with his recommendation that the Constituent Assembly have the power to release an imprisoned delegate.[35] His party was always hostile to the terrorists, whose military operations were not directed by the Haganah but by the Irgun and

[30] *M.H.H. Proceedings,* twenty-sixth meeting, p. 21.
[31] *Ibid.,* p. 24.
[32] *Ibid.,* twenty-eighth meeting, p. 26.
[33] *'Iton Rishmi,* No. 33, Supp. 1, November 19, 1948, p. 58.
[34] *M.H.H. Proceedings,* twenty-seventh meeting, pp. 17-18.
[35] *Ibid.,* p. 19.

Sternists—two military organizations which the Kneset Israel was never able to control.

Soldiers too were to vote, but a separate ordinance restricted campaigning in the army.[36] There were virtually no restrictions on the mailing of campaign literature to soldiers. Public meetings were prohibited, though soldiers could be given passes, furloughs, and leaves to attend or participate in the meetings of civilians. Soldiers were eligible to become candidates and, if elected, were to be separated from the service until after the Constituent Assembly had concluded its sessions.

The State Council fixed January 25, 1949, as the date for the elections.[37]

OTHER LEGISLATION REGARDING CONSTITUENT ASSEMBLY

A decree was approved by the State Council which provided for the functioning of the Government in the interim between its own expiration and the establishment of a new authority by the Constituent Assembly.[38] The debate[39] was interesting in that it revealed the Provisional Government's anticipation that the Constituent Assembly would become the legislative body of the State, from which the executive authority would be constituted. It also revealed how much doubt there was that a formal constitution would be drafted.

Several members of the Council wanted to set a limit on the term of the Constituent Assembly. They wanted it to have two years within which to draft a constitution, or at most four. The Provisional Government opposed any limit whatever and prevailed. It argued legalistically that the State Council had no power to restrict the first democratically elected organ of the state—the Constituent Assembly. The debate indicated that many already felt that the Constituent Assembly would not be

[36] *'Iton Rishmi*, No. 38, Supp. 1, December 17, 1948, pp. 81-82.
[37] *Ibid.*, No. 34, November 26, 1948, p. 100.
[38] *Ibid.*, No. 42, Supp. 1, January 14, 1949, pp. 105-6.
[39] *M.H.H. Proceedings*, thirty-sixth meeting, pp. 5-12.

that in fact but what it actually became—the First Kneset—the first popularly elected legislative body to succeed the State Council. Furthermore, rules and procedures in the Constituent Assembly, until changed, were to be the same as those that prevailed in the State Council.

That this debate took place before the elections meant that voters had sufficient indication of the role the Assembly might play. The Provisional Government was also expected to function until a successor government was chosen from the Constituent Assembly. Thus the voters also knew that a new executive authority would be constituted from the Assembly.

One other phase of the debate is of interest. It was suggested that the eldest of the delegates elected to the Constituent Assembly call it to order. The Government, on the other hand, insisted that the president of the Provisional Government do so. A majority in the Council sustained the latter point of view.[40]

BENIGN EFFECTS OF PARTY UNITY

Israel waged its war for independence during the period of the Provisional Government. Perhaps, therefore, because it was a period of maximum national unity and minimum party strife, the achievements of the Provisional Government were quantitatively and qualitatively superior to the achievements of the First Kneset that followed.

The small State Council was virtually a committee of the whole, not merely on legislation but on much that later would be classified as administrative regulation. The ministers were active in lawmaking despite their preoccupation with the organization of their departments, but the ordinances or decrees proposed by them received the benefit of truly constructive criticism. The legislators were less concerned with embarrassing a coalition government and more concerned with the successful prosecution of the war, its financing, and the shaping of the political, economic,

[40] *Ibid.*, p. 9.

and social institutions of the new state. Thus the military crisis, and the tensions and enthusiasms it engendered, had a benign effect on the establishment of the Government. One has reason to wonder whether as much could have been accomplished if peace had prevailed and the interparty hostility had reigned as usual.

The First Kneset, which succeeded the State Council, was three times as large and more inclined to debating. Its Executive was constituted from fewer parties. Therefore, the opposition in the legislature had to make political capital of all the faults it could find. The Executive, in turn, was impelled to draw away as much as possible from the lawmakers. It operated less as a team with the group from among whom it was constituted and more as an independent branch. While it cannot be said that it was less dedicated to the public good, it had to become more conscious of party considerations, which inspired altogether too much Kneset debate.

CHAPTER V

The Transition Law

THE 1949 ELECTION RESULTS

The elections to the Constituent Assembly took place on January 25, 1949. Twenty-one lists of candidates had been nominated, though not all the lists set forth 120 candidates.[1]

Of nine lists with a combined vote of 19,424, not one candidate was elected.[2] The remaining parties won seats as follows: Mapai, 46; Mapam, 19; United Religious Bloc, 16; Herut, 14; General Zionists, 7; Progressives, 5; Sephardim, 4; Communists, 4; Democratic of Nazareth (Arab), 2; Fighters, 1; WIZO, 1; and Yemenites, 1.[3]

The Assembly convened in Jerusalem on February 14, 1949. A day later, the Committee on Credentials (Wa'adat ha-Mandatim) reported no challenges to the eligibility or election of its members,[4] and the Committee on the Constitution—which had prepared a transition law—reported on February 16.[5] The members of these committees had been nominated by the Permanent Committee, which consisted of 33 members who were representative of all the parties in the Constituent Assembly.[6] Voting in the Permanent Committee was proportional to party strength in

[1] A. Zidon, *ha-Kneset* (Tel Aviv, 5710), p. 43.
[2] *Ibid.*, p. 46.
[3] *Ibid.*, p. 45. The procedure is described *supra*, pp. 58-59.
[4] *Divrei ha-Kneset*, I, 1st Sess., 3d meeting, 25.
[5] *Ibid.*, 4th meeting, p. 28.
[6] Zidon, *ha-Kneset*, p. 57.

the Assembly,[7] as was the case in the State Council's committee to prepare the elections decree.

On February 16, Chaim Weizmann was elected to the presidency. The Provisional Government tendered its resignation on the day following. The names of the members of the new Government[8] were submitted on March 8, and a vote of confidence was won on March 10.[9]

PROVISIONS PERTAINING TO THE KNESET

The Committee on the Constitution, appointed by the State Council, had prepared drafts of two articles on the legislative and executive authorities.[10] A briefer version of them became the Transition Law[11] approved by Israel's Constituent Assembly on February 16, 1949. By the terms of this law the Constituent Assembly became the First Kneset, or legislature, of the new State, in which capacity it functioned until the summer of 1951.[12]

The change from Constituent Assembly to Kneset was accomplished virtually without protest. As a matter of fact, the move was anticipated even before the elections, and after the elections no political party expected to gain any advantage by insisting upon the immediate drafting of a constitution and a new election in accordance with its provisions.

[7] *Ibid.*

[8] The portfolios were distributed as follows:
David Ben Gurion (Mapai), Head of Government and Defense.
Dov Joseph (Mapai), Supply and Budget.
Yizhaq Meir Lewin (U.R.B.), Welfare.
Golda Meyerson (Mapai), Labor and Social Security.
Judah Leib Maimon (U.R.B.), Religion.
Eli'ezer Kaplan (Mapai), Finance.
David Remez (Mapai), Communications.
Pinhas Rosen (Progressives), Justice.
Bekhor Shalom Shitreet (Sephardim), Police.
Zalman Shazar (Mapai), Education and Culture.
Moshe Shapiro (U.R.B.), Interior and Immigration.
Moshe Sharet (Mapai), Foreign Affairs.

[9] *Divrei ha-Kneset,* I, 1st Sess., 12th meeting, 142-44.

[10] *W.H. Proceedings,* Pamphlets III and IV.

[11] *Sefer ha-Huqim, 5709,* pp. 1-2.

[12] Elections for the Second Kneset were held on July 30, 1951.

However, no term was specified for the First Kneset.[13] Nor were there provisions for a new election even in the event of a cabinet crisis. The president was given no power to call for an election and apparently only the Kneset itself could do so. As a result, so long as a coalition government could be organized, the Kneset retained legislative power.[14] The people, whose numbers were rapidly increasing, might have been deprived of a chance to elect new representatives for a long time to come. However, a disagreement within the coalition in 1951 and the inability of the Head of the Government to organize another coalition made new elections necessary. For the Second Kneset a term of four years was fixed.[15]

Only two paragraphs of the fifteen contained in the Transition Law deal with the legislature, while five deal with the president and five with the Government. The remaining three amended prior laws, established the official gazette, *Reshumot,* and fixed the effective date of the Transition Law.

The first paragraph gives the name "Kneset" to the legislature; it calls the Constituent Assembly the "First Kneset," and every delegate "Haver ha-Kneset" (Member of the Kneset). The second paragraph calls every legislative act of the Kneset a "Hoq" (law).[16] Every law is to be signed by the Head of the Government and the "Sar" (minister) competent to execute it. The president too must sign all the laws except those concerning his prerogatives,[17] and within ten days after their enactment by the

[13] To this Mr. Vilner of the Communist Party objected but he was overruled (*Divrei ha-Kneset,* I, 1st Session, 4th meeting, 32-33).

[14] This was the status of the law even when the Head of the Government, on November 21, 1949, assured the Kneset that new elections would be held not later than 1953 (*Divrei ha-Kneset,* III, 2d Sess., 87th meeting, 128). He was merely expressing his intention, not the legal situation.

[15] *Sefer ha-Huqim, 5711,* p. 104.

[16] This name was reserved for laws of the Kneset and that is why the laws of the State Council of the Provisional Government were called "pequdot" (decrees). See *Shenaton ha-Memshalah, 5710,* p. 5.

[17] It was understood that the purpose of the signature was solely to establish the law's authenticity (*Divrei ha-Kneset,* I, 1st Sess., 4th meeting, 33).

Kneset, each shall be published in the *Official Gazette,* the name of which was changed by paragraph 13 to *Reshumot.*

These two paragraphs on the legislature are a far cry from the twenty-eight sections which the Committee on the Constitution had prepared as their proposal for an article on the same subject in a projected constitution.[18] The twenty-eight sections included provisions with regard to the eligibility of the members themselves (secs. 2 and 3). The size of the legislature was fixed (sec. 4*b*) and the manner (sec. 4*a*) and time (sec. 5) of its election. Its term (sec. 8) also was established and the number of its annual sessions (sec. 7). Between sessions a permanent committee of one-fourth of the members of the legislature would sit (sec. 7*c*), and special sessions could be convened by the president, the Government, or one-third of the legislators (sec. 7*d*). The president was given the power to adjourn the body, but not more often than once during its term (sec. 9). Open and free debate (secs. 12 and 16) in the legislature was provided for, and publication of the debates was also assured immunity (sec. 10*b*). The legislature was authorized to fix its own rules of procedure (sec. 11*a*). One speaker and two vice-speakers were to be elected to serve for the full term (sec. 11, *b* and *c*), but the legislature itself could determine the number, composition, and authority of its committees (sec. 11*d*). The rights and privileges of the legislators were set forth as well as the limitations imposed upon them (secs. 17, 18, and 19). The legislative process was defined (secs. 20, 21, and 22) and the method of approving the budget (secs. 24 and 25). The legislature was given the power to tax (sec. 26*a*), incur indebtedness, and alienate the State's property (sec. 26*b*). It was also given the power to conscript (sec. 27), declare war (sec. 28*a*), and ratify treaties of peace as well as other international covenants or agreements (sec. 28*b*).

Though none of these sections was included in the Transition

[18] *W.H. Proceedings,* Pamphlet III, pp. 60-70.

Law, several were included in decrees of the State Council[19] and in statutes approved by the Kneset,[20] or became parliamentary patterns,[21] so that it cannot be said that the committee's effort was in vain. Furthermore, all the powers that the committee would have granted to the legislature were actually exercised by it. Shortly before its dissolution, however, the First Kneset also defined the rights and duties as well as the immunities and privileges of the legislators.[22]

PROVISIONS PERTAINING TO THE PRESIDENT

With regard to the president, the Transition Law is considerably more specific than with regard to the Kneset.

Chapter two of the Transition Law reads as follows:

3. Election of President.
    (a) The president of the state shall be elected by the Kneset by secret ballot.
    (b) The candidate who receives more than half the votes of all the members of the Kneset shall be the elected one.
    (c) Should no candidate receive such a majority, a second ballot shall be taken. If such a majority does not result from the second ballot, a further ballot shall be taken. On the third ballot and each successive ballot that candidate will be dropped who received on the ballot preceding the smallest number of votes. The candidate who on the third or any succeeding ballot receives more than half the number of votes of the members voting shall be deemed elected.
4. President's Declaration.
    Within seven days of his election, the president shall deliver

[19] E.g., the age qualification of voters for members of the legislature and the age qualification of candidates themselves were included in the elections decree. See *supra*, p. 60.

[20] E.g., members of the legislature were prohibited from receiving salaries from any source other than as members thereof (*Sefer ha-Huqim, 5709*, p. 42 [sec. 8]).

[21] E.g., the election of one chairman and two vice-chairmen of the Kneset. See *infra*, p. 101.

[22] *Sefer ha-Huqim, 5711*, pp. 228-30.

and sign in the Kneset or before the Chairman of the Kneset this declaration: "I (name), as president of the state, pledge allegiance to the State of Israel and its laws."

5. President's Term of Office.

The term of office of the president of the state shall extend for the life of the first Kneset and for three months following the assembling of a new Kneset.

6. President's Duties.

The president of the state shall sign treaties with foreign states which have been ratified by the Kneset, appoint on the recommendation of the authorized minister the diplomatic representatives of the state, receive the diplomatic representatives of foreign states sent to Israel and confirm the appointment of consuls of foreign states; the authority to pardon offenders and mitigate punishments is also vested in him.

7. President's Signature.

Every official act signed by the president shall bear one confirmatory signature of the Head of the Government or of such other minister as shall be decided on by the Government.

How do these sections compare with related provisions in Dr. Kohn's draft and the proposals of the Committee on the Constitution? Dr. Kohn, in his draft, had proposed a section to the effect that "The executive power in the State of Isreal shall be vested in the president of the Republic and in the Executive Council."[23] The members of the committee—all of whom were committed to the greater desirability of the parliamentary form of government for Israel—feared that such a section might give rise to the impression that it established an executive branch of the government, comparable to that provided for in the federal Constitution of the United States. For that reason the committee found unacceptable even Professor Vitta's suggestion that the section read that the executive power be vested in the president who shall exercise it by means of the Head of the Government and a number of ministers.[24] However, Dr. Wahrhaftig's view prevailed. The

[23] *W. H. Proceedings*, Pamphlet II, Article 48.

[24] *Ibid.*, Pamphlet V, p. 47.

section was omitted altogether by the committee, and the Transition Law reflects the same conclusion.

The committee, however, had discussed qualifications for the office of president, which Chapter two of the Transition Law also failed to mention. Recommendations for the minimum age of the president ranged from thirty to forty. But the issue most warmly debated by the committee was whether the president had to be a Jew.[25] Grabovsky pleaded that such a requirement would embarrass Jews in other lands. The inclusion of a "racist" idea in the Israeli constitution would give other nations an argument which they might use in the event Israel should seek to uphold the rights of Jews residing among them.

Harari agreed with Grabovsky, adding that there is no agreement as to who is a Jew. One might claim that an irreligious Jew is not worthy of the title.[26] Wahrhaftig did not think Grabovsky's fears were justified. He claimed that in other respects the constitution would favor Jews. Only Jews would have an unrestricted right of immigration. Only the Jews who might come to Israel would enjoy almost instantaneous citizenship. Why then should a Jewish state hesitate to make it clear that her "first citizen," the symbol of her independence, is a Jew? At any event, he felt the section was not necessary and, since a debate on the subject could only cause embarrassment, it might be best to leave it out altogether.[27]

Loewenstein regarded such an attitude as cowardice. He wanted a specific requirement that the president be a Jew. He urged his colleagues not to worry about the "racist" idea, saying "Because of our race we were hounded and because of our race we are alive."[28]

Weinstein agreed with Wahrhaftig that the omission of the section altogether was the best solution.[29]

With regard to the manner of electing the president, there was

[25] *Ibid.*, Pamphlet IV, pp. 7-8. [26] *Ibid.*, p. 7.
[27] *Ibid.*, pp. 7-8. [28] *Ibid.*, p. 8. [29] *Ibid.*

also disagreement in the committee. The Revisionist spokesman favored an election by the people. He felt that such a direct election would really place the president above party consideration.[30] Nominations might be, as Dr. Kohn had proposed,[31] by the petition of twenty-five members of the legislature, or by five municipal councils. The committee, however, did not agree. They felt that a popular election would only make the president feel that as the people's tribune he must assert himself in opposition to the legislature.[32]

Yet, if the Kneset is to elect the president, the problem is how to attain a real majority. Grabovsky thought that there might be resort to a popular election should a candidate fail to get at least a majority vote of the legislators participating in the vote.[33] Even that concession to the people was disapproved. The committee did approve, however, of what became section 3 of Chapter two of the Transition Law.[34]

The committee considered the oath to be taken by the president on entering office and the persons in whose presence it should be taken. With regard to the oath itself, the "religious" members of the committee were to prepare one that would be acceptable to the religious groups.[35] Professor Vitta had recommended that, instead of an oath to support the laws of Israel, the oath should be to support the laws of the State of Israel. Otherwise one might assume that the reference was to all the laws of Judaism.[36]

Kohn had proposed a term of five years for the president and his re-eligibility for but one additional term.[37] Vitta proposed a six-year term, with no mention of eligibility or ineligibility for a second term.[38] The committee divided. Wahrhaftig and Grabov-

[30] *Ibid.*

[31] *Ibid.*, p. 38, Professor Vitta had suggested a percentage, e.g. 25 percent of the legislature rather than a specific number (*ibid.*, Pamphlet V, pp. 19, 46).

[32] *Ibid.*, Pamphlet IV, p. 9.

[33] *Ibid.*, p. 10.

[34] *Ibid.*, p. 11.

[35] *Ibid.*, p. 16.

[36] *Ibid.*, Pamphlet V, p. 19.

[37] *Ibid.*, Pamphlet IV, p. 39.

[38] *Ibid.*, Pamphlet V, pp. 19, 46.

sky favored a presidential term which would exceed the fixed term of the Kneset, though occasionally the terms of all would expire simultaneously.[39] Nir and Loewenstein favored a term for the president equal to that of the legislature.[40] All agreed, however, that the president should be eligible to succeed himself for only one additional term, though he might be elected again to succeed someone else.[41]

Grabovsky sought to except the first president from any limitations whatever.[42] Wahrhaftig pointed out that Czechoslovakia in 1920 honored Masaryk in this way.[43] However, no one voted with Grabovsky on this recommendation.[44]

Section 5 of Chapter two of the Transition Law provided only for a term that would expire three months following the inauguration of a newly elected legislature. However, the enumeration of the president's powers in section 6 was considerably shorter than in the sections proposed by the committee.[45]

That the president was to have very limited power was a foregone conclusion. Dr. Kohn had argued[46] against giving the president powers equal to those of the president of the United States. He also disapproved of the extension of the presidential powers according to the Weimar Constitution, which not only gave the president a veto power but enabled him to conduct referenda. He argued that the extension of the presidential powers in Germany by the Weimar Constitution caused its ruin. The president was able to destroy parliament and rule by executive decree.[47] The committee accepted this general view, but it did vote to give the president the power to convoke special sessions of the legislature, to dissolve it, and to confirm the appointment of the supreme commander of the armed forces. However, these were omitted from section 6 of Chapter two of the Transition Law.[48]

[39] *Ibid.*, Pamphlet IV, p. 13. [40] *Ibid.* [41] *Ibid.* [42] *Ibid.* [43] *Ibid.*
[44] *Ibid.* [45] *Ibid.*, pp. 40-41. [46] *Ibid.*, Pamphlet II, p. 32. [47] *Ibid.*
[48] The Kneset later passed a law providing that it may be reconvened during a recess by the Government or by petition of 40 members (*Sefer ha-Huqim, 5709*, p. 295).

Professor Vitta made an additional suggestion that the power to pardon should not apply to general amnesties, which should only be declared by the Kneset.[49] The recommendation was not accepted by the committee. However, section 6 of Chapter two of the Transition Law, which refers to "pardoning offenders," does not specify whether general amnesties are included.

The committee agreed on the following section: "Every official act of the president of the state shall bear the countersignature of the Head of the Government who will thereby assume responsibility for it."[50]

Dr. Kohn had recommended the countersignature of either the Head of the Government or a member of the Executive Council,[51] and section 7 of Chapter two of the Transition Law provided for the countersignature of the Head of the Government or such other Minister as shall be decided by the Government.

The Committee on the Constitution considered and proposed many other sections concerning the president. These included the time when the Kneset must elect a president; who would succeed him in the event of death, resignation, disability, or removal; the manner of determining his disability, and the manner of impeaching and trying him.[52] It would appear that the Kneset was satisfied to have such decisions made when the emergencies arose. And on April 6, 1949,[53] it did pass a temporary law making the presiding officer of the Kneset the acting president of the State during the president's absence from Israel. This did not mean, however, that the presiding officer of the Kneset would have to discontinue his functions as such.

PROVISIONS PERTAINING TO THE GOVERNMENT

Chapter three of the Transition Law deals with "The Government" which is Israel's cabinet.

[49] *W.H. Proceedings*, Pamphlet V, p. 21.
[50] *Ibid.*, Pamphlet IV, p. 19. [51] *Ibid.*, p. 41. [52] *Ibid.*, pp. 39, 41.
[53] *Sefer ha-Huqim, 5709*, p. 8. See also *ibid.*, p. 72, and *Sefer ha-Huqim, 5710*, p. 157.

Section 8 of this chapter called for the resignation of the Provisional Government immediately after the election of the president, though it was to serve until a new Government was established. However, even the terminology used in this section, as well as all the remaining provisions of the chapter, received considerable attention.

Dr. Kohn, in his draft, had proposed the term "Executive Council" for what is usually called the cabinet—presumably because many Europeans and Americans take the term "Government" to mean the total machinery of the state. Nonetheless, the Committee on the Constitution preferred "Government" to describe the executive authority comprising the Head of the Government, the ministers who are heads of departments, and ministers without portfolio.[54] The Transition Law also employed that term. There was also some disagreement about the Hebrew word for minister. Dr. Kohn in his draft used the word "Sar"—normally translated "officer." Vilner, the internationalist, preferred "minister," a Hebraized form of the international word.[55] Grabovsky suggested "Naggid," a historic Hebrew title of distinction.[56] Wahrhaftig[57] agreed with Kohn, and the Transition Law uses the word "Sar."

All of this, however, was not as significant as two other issues: Who should choose the ministers and should they be chosen exclusively from the legislature?

Dr. Kohn had proposed that only legislators be eligible for the Government, as in England.[58] He also suggested a maximum of fifteen men. The Government might, of course, seek the advice of experts, but unless the head of a department is also a legislator he should not be given major responsibility for carrying out the mandate of the legislature, nor would his *expertise* qualify him

[54] *W.H. Proceedings*, Pamphlet IV, p. 22. [55] *Ibid.*, p. 23.
[56] *Ibid.* [57] *Ibid.*
[58] *Ibid.*, Pamphlet II, p. 33. Shertok, however, disagreed (*Divrei ha-Kneset*, I, 1st Sess., 4th meeting, 39-40). In England the rule is one of usage, not law.

for parliamentary debate in which he might have to engage.[59] Vitta disagreed,[60] saying that if the chamber was not satisfied with the choice of heads of departments they had their remedy, and, furthermore, these experts were very often excellent parliamentarians and even party leaders, though they were not elected to the legislature. The committee agreed with Vitta, Grabovsky dissenting.[61] Moreover, they accepted[62] Vitta's suggestion[63] that no specific number of ministers be set forth.

The committee agreed that ministers should be chosen by the Head of the Government. The president, after consultation with the party leaders would appoint the Head of the Government, who in turn would select the men with whom he felt he would have an efficient team. Kohn and Vitta agreed on this.[64] Kohn expressed his disapproval of the method prevailing in the Irish Free State, whereby the Parliament elects every minister.[65]

Consequently the Committee on the Constitution approved two sections, which became sections 9 and 10 of the Transition Law, as follows:

9. Duty of Forming Government.

After consultation with representatives of the parties in the Kneset, the president of the state shall assign to one of the members of the Kneset the task of forming a Government.

10. Government's Composition.

The Government shall be composed of a Head of the Government and a number of ministers from among the members of the Kneset or from outside[66] [the Kneset].

The next problem was that of the responsibility of the Govern-

[59] *W.H. Proceedings,* Pamphlet II, p. 33. [60] *Ibid.,* Pamphlet V, p. 22.
[61] *Ibid.,* Pamphlet IV, p. 23. [62] *Ibid.* [63] *Ibid.,* Pamphlet V, p. 21.
[64] *Ibid.,* Pamphlet II, p. 33, and Pamphlet V, p. 22.
[65] *Ibid.,* Pamphlet II, p. 33. Harari also disapproved of the system whereby each party in the coalition designates its choice for the cabinet. He argued that since the Head of the Government must form a Government that will win a vote of confidence, the parties are not without power, but the Head of the Government should have as free a hand as is possible.
[66] A minister who is not a member of the Kneset enjoys all the rights and privileges of a member of the Kneset except for the right to vote (*Divrei ha-Kneset,* VII, 3d Sess., 191st meeting, 248-51).

ment, its accountability, and its resignation or removal. Dr. Kohn had proposed the British pattern, by which the Head of the Government is the pivot around which everything revolves. If he were to resign because he had failed to win a vote of confidence, the entire Government would go with him.[67] On this the committee agreed.[68]

Furthermore, the Committee agreed[69] that "The Government shall function in accordance with the policies approved by the Chamber of Deputies";[70] and "The Government shall be responsible collectively for all its acts to the Chamber of Deputies and every minister shall be individually responsible for the acts of his department."

The substance of these decisions was included in the first three paragraphs of section 11 of the Transition Law:

(a) The Government, immediately after it has been constituted, shall appear before the Kneset, and shall be deemed formed after having received a vote of confidence.
(b) Within seven days from the day that the Government received a vote of confidence, the Head of the Government and the other ministers shall read and sign before the Kneset this declaration: "I (name), as a member of the Government, pledge allegiance to the State of Israel and its Laws and to carry out the decisions of the Kneset."
(c) The Government shall be collectively responsible for its acts to the Kneset, shall report to the Kneset on them, and shall continue in office so long as it enjoys the confidence of the Kneset.

The last paragraph of section 11 of the Transition Law provided for the resignation of a Government:

4. A Government in which the Kneset has voted no-confidence, or which has decided to resign, shall forthwith tender its resignation to the president of the state. However, it shall continue its functions

[67] *W.H. Proceedings*, Pamphlet II, p. 33.
[68] *Ibid.*, Pamphlet IV, p. 25. [69] *Ibid.*
[70] The Committee on the Constitution used Dr. Kohn's term for the legislature.

until the establishment of a new Government pursuant to the provisions of this law.

This paragraph is a brief substitute for the elaborate provisions debated and recommended by the Committee on the Constitution regarding the manner in which votes of confidence or no-confidence shall be proposed and the number of votes necessary to achieve the resignation of the Government.

Professor Vitta, for example, had suggested[71] that the proposal for a vote of no-confidence should be submitted to the Kneset at least three days in advance of the vote and only upon the written request of at least 25 percent of the members present at the session. The proposal should set forth the reasons therefor. The Government should be able to request a vote of confidence at any time, but must do so within ten days after it is organized. To deny the Government's request for a vote of confidence, or to pass a legislator's motion for no confidence, should require a majority of *all* the legislators. Only then should the Government resign.

Vilner suggested that if the Government requested the vote of confidence it too should be required to win a majority vote of all the legislators or resign.[72]

Wahrhaftig expressed strong opposition to the view that the constitution must fix all details in accordance with the patterns of other states, without giving Israel the chance to develop her own parliamentary methods and institutions. He felt that the constitution need only provide for the general principle that the Government must receive a vote of confidence from the legislature and can serve only so long as it enjoys this confidence. Even the coalition government of Israel—and before it the Jewish Agency—was more than a coalition. There were always programs and goals on which all members of the coalition were united. The Government was therefore always more than an artificial union of party heads. Why then try to ape France? Let

[71] *Ibid.*, Pamphlet V, pp. 22, 48. [72] *Ibid.*, Pamphlet IV, p. 29.

Israel develop her own procedures on votes of confidence. For the constitution to set forth the principle was enough.[73]

Wahrhaftig, however, did feel that a resigning Government should function until a successor Government was chosen. To this Nir objected, for a conspiracy by the outgoing Government might prevent a new one from coming into being.[74] Wahrhaftig's view on both issues prevailed in the First Kneset, as evidenced by paragraph 4 of section 11 of the Transition Law.

Vitta had also proposed that there be added a section authorizing the Minister of Justice to act instead of the Head of the Government in the event of the latter's temporary disability or absence, and authorizing the Head of the Government to appoint anyone to act instead of a minister who is temporarily disabled or absent.[75] The proposal was accepted later, and in the absence of Ben Gurion the Ministers of Justice and Finance have in fact acted in his stead.

Kohn had recommended a clause to the effect that no minister may be a member of the board of directors of any joint stock or limited liability company carrying on business for profit.[76] The committee agreed in principle but felt that the clause did not go far enough;[77] ministers should not be allowed to be active in the affairs or management of any business for profit.

The debate was interesting because of the questions raised. What of a member of a cooperative colony? What of a professional man? What of a stockholder in a corporation? What about civil servants? The committee agreed that the constitution need not deal with civil servants[78]—the Kneset could deal with that by statute. But Grabovsky of Mapai was concerned that a member of a cooperative be eligible to be a minister while Weinstein, the Revisionist, was concerned that a corporate stockholder be thus eligible.

[73] *Ibid.*, p. 27. [74] *Ibid.*
[75] *W.H. Proceedings*, Pamphlet V, pp. 23, 48.
[76] *Ibid.*, Pamphlet II, p. 13. [77] *Ibid.*, Pamphlet IV, p. 32.
[78] *Ibid.*, p. 33.

The First Kneset acted upon this recommendation only to the extent of prohibiting members of the Kneset from receiving any salary other than as members of the Kneset.[79] It did not, however, act upon many other recommendations pertaining to the immunity of ministers to criminal prosecution, their impeachment, the manner of trying them, the establishment of a civil service commission for competitive examinations,[80] and the right of civil servants to organize and strike.

INADEQUACY OF THE TRANSITION LAW

The Transition Law assured the continuance of the parliamentary form of government. However, it was hardly a substitute for a constitution, though often called Israel's small one. The legislative process was not described at all. The judiciary was not even mentioned. Limitations on the legislature were nil. There was not even a guarantee that the legislature would not become a self-perpetuating oligarchy.

It is amazing that the Transition Law did not create alarm by its utter failure to safeguard democracy by periodic elections —not to mention the safeguarding of specific human rights and fundamental freedoms. Either Israelis had such faith in their legislators that they did not fear a coup d'état, or they knew from the intense hostility between party leaders that the latter regarded a lasting coalition as beyond the realm of possibility. Yet it may be that written constitutions simply did not loom significant in their eyes. Established usage was more important, and established usage gave them a sense of security.

[79] *Sefer ha-Huqim, 5709,* p. 42.

[80] The Government did in fact appoint such a commission consisting of five persons. Two it itself nominated, and the remaining three were nominated by the Supreme Court, the Senate of the Hebrew University, and the Teachers Council of the Technion. See S. Malik, and M. Nurock, "Takhnit ha-Behinot le-'Ovdei Medinat Yisrael" (The Examinations Program for Israel's Civil Servants), *ha-Minahel,* No. 5 (Spring, 1951), pp. 9-13.

CHAPTER VI

Constitutional Principles of the First Kneset

On March 10, 1949, the Kneset ratified its Fundamental Principles,[1] many of which have great constitutional significance.

JOINT RESPONSIBILITY

The first section dealt with the executive authority, the "Government." It set forth the joint responsibility of all the cabinet members, and the parties they represent, for all that the Government did. This was a restatement of paragraph 11*c* of the Transition Law. Nonetheless, members of the Kneset were to enjoy complete freedom of debate on every measure proposed, and might even criticize the Government for any deviation from policies determined by itself or the Kneset. They were not estopped from such criticism because their party was represented in the Government.

This was the section on which the Head of the Government relied when he felt impelled to submit the resignation of the entire Government before making a few changes in its personnel.[2] After the resignation of the old Government a new one could be formed with the changes sought. To make individual changes, however, might have flouted the principle of joint and collective

[1] *Divrei ha-Kneset,* I, 1st Sess., 7th meeting, 55-56. The principles were included in a report by the Head of the Government to the Kneset, which report was fully debated and approved.

[2] *Ibid.,* VII, 3d Sess., 179th meeting, 8. This practice was changed by the Second Kneset.

responsibility. This was also the section on which he had relied the year before to compel ministers who boycotted cabinet meetings to attend, lest their continued absence be regarded as their resignation.[3]

BILL OF RIGHTS

The second section set forth the "democratic, republican" character of the state. Complete equality of rights and duties was guaranteed to all citizens without discrimination because of creed, race, or nationality. Freedom of religion, conscience, language, education, and culture was also assured. For women too there was to be established full and complete equality in political, social, and economic affairs with respect to both rights and duties. The laws were also to assure freedom of association and freedom of expression—oral and written—with due regard to the security of the State, her freedom and independence, as well as respect for personal rights. In all the State's institutions, including municipal ones, and elected agencies the right of general and equal voting was to be without discrimination because of sex, creed, race, or nationality, and there were to be no property qualifications. The State was to provide for the religious needs of her inhabitants while herself refraining from performing religious functions, though one can hardly reconcile this principle with the Israeli system of state-supported ecclesiastical courts which enjoy exclusive jurisdiction over many matters. The Sabbaths and Jewish festivals were to be fixed days of rest, but non-Jews were to have the privilege of observing their own Sabbaths and festivals.

This section was virtually a Bill of Rights. Its last two sentences were relevant to the problem of religion in the State, which will be discussed in a separate chapter.[4] Suffice it to say that the

[3] *Ibid.*, IV, 2d Sess., 118th meeting, 830.
[4] See *infra*, Chapter IX.

state was empowered to support religion while not itself engaging in religious work.[5]

This section, however, did not bar discrimination in the matter of providing for the religious needs of all of the inhabitants. Was the omission purposeful? Could Arab and Christian communities have claimed support on the same basis provided for the religious life of the Jewish communities? Or did the state have the power to discriminate? Could it even discriminate as between different Jewish denominations—if there were more than one in Israel, as in America? Or was the language of the section broad enough to require the fulfillment of the religious requirements of all inhabitants? The Government has already expended funds on the religious courts of the non-Jewish religious communities for the rehabilitation of their places of worship and cemeteries and for the establishment of schools for their children. However, since the practice of the many faiths differs, it may be impossible to think of complete equality of treatment. The Government, for example, need not make an appropriation for the observance of dietary laws by Christians. Perhaps that is why a nondiscrimination clause was regarded as inapplicable to a situation where difference in treatment is almost of its essence. Thus, while the Government permits Protestant churches to broadcast their services—even in Hebrew —they must not include any material that would constitute an affront to the religious feelings of other denominations. The fear is that the Protestants may use the broadcasts for missionary purposes. No such restriction is placed on Jewish services, perhaps because Judaism is no longer a missionary religion. At any event, the difficulty of a nondiscrimination clause regarding religion becomes apparent. Nonetheless the question of discrimina-

[5] This is not the American pattern, although the new position of the Roman Catholic Church with regard to the support of American parochial schools would seem to indicate that its newest position is reflected in this section. It would like government subsidies for its schools without the state becoming involved in religious affairs.

tion in favor of Judaism was raised in the Kneset in the debate on the first budget for its religious communities.[6]

It should also be pointed out that the Government did not obligate itself to provide for a man's private religious needs. The term "religious needs" was qualified in the section by the word "public." Presumably only the needs of organized religious communities were intended. However, the obligation was incurred for "inhabitants"—not for citizens exclusively.[7] Did Israel thus undertake to care for religious functionaries who did not become citizens and remained in the land only because of its historic associations, without any sympathy whatever for either the program or the goals of the new republic? By contrast with this, the complete equality guaranteed in the first sentence of the section applied only to "citizens." This limitation represented a deviation from Dr. Kohn's draft which assured equal rights to "all persons" within the State's jurisdiction and limited only civic and political rights to citizens.

FOREIGN POLICY

The third section dealt with Israel's foreign policy. It called for adherence to the principles of the United Nations Charter and friendship with all peace-loving peoples—particularly with the United States and the Soviet Union.

It called also for effort to the end that there might come into being between Israel and all neighboring Muslim states treaties involving political, cultural, social, and economic cooperation—all within the framework of the United Nations.[8]

Lastly, Israel undertook to support every move that would in-

[6] *Divrei ha-Kneset,* II, 1st Sess., 67th meeting, 1304.

[7] See E. M. Million and A. S. Katz, "Provisions on Religious Freedom in the Draft Israeli Constitution—a Comparative Study," *New York University Law Quarterly Review,* No. 24 (1949), pp. 846-84.

[8] The treaties, however, were not to constitute an alliance against anyone in the United Nations. Israel sought to maintain the much coveted "neutrality" between East and West. A regional alliance was not to become like other "unions" in Europe or Asia.

sure world peace and promote human rights and the equality of sovereign states as well as strengthen the authority and efficacy of the United Nations.

What these principles of "neutrality" and "support of the United Nations" have meant in practice can be gleaned from the votes and speeches of Israel's representatives in the United Nations after admission to membership in that organization. Obviously the two principles often came into conflict. Neutrality required that Israel abstain from voting on numerous issues on which East and West were divided. This she did. However, contributing to stalemates was not helping the United Nations to become strong. And Israel did express views even when she abstained from voting. She was not altogether passive. And her views were geared principally to advancing "the efficacy and the reputation of the World Organization."[9]

As part of its foreign policy, Israel guaranteed an immigration visa to every Jew desirous of settling in the land of Israel. This guarantee was contained in Dr. Kohn's draft of a constitution and became the butt of considerable criticism abroad.[10] This section also called for effective vigilance over the full independence and sovereignty of the State.

CONSCRIPTION

The power to conscript was affirmed in general terms in the fourth section. Later statutes were to be more specific. The principal problem in this connection, however, was the conscription of women, to which the Religious Bloc was opposed.[11]

[9] See S. Arad, "Israel and the United Nations," *Jewish Frontier*, XVII, No. 4 (April, 1950), 30. Israel's support of the United Nations in Korea was opposed by the Communist and Mapam parties. See *Divrei ha-Kneset*, VI, 2d Sess., 161st meeting, 2058-86; *ibid.*, 174th meeting, 2419-21; *ibid.*, 176 meeting, 2506-7.

[10] See *infra*, p. 155.

[11] See *infra*, p. 151, for a discussion of the temporary compromise achieved and its failure, causing the issue to become a critical one in 1951.

ABSORPTION OF IMMIGRANTS

The fifth and sixth sections dealt with the absorption of immigrants, calling for their housing and education as well as their cultural and economic assimilation. From a constitutional point of view their significance lay in the fact that the State had assumed complete responsibility for every detail. But, in addition to assuming the responsibility, the sections set forth a number of specific projects for the development of the land and its resources. As a result several lesser constitutional principles were asserted. There was to be no confiscation of private property for public use without compensation. Yet, the Government was empowered to force private owners to develop their lands by discriminatory taxation. The Government was also to promote means of communication and transport.

Government control over the economy was to extend to the curbing of inflation, control of imports, profits, foreign exchange, and consumption of goods. Graduated income and inheritance taxes were approved. The promotion of health, social security, and even the breakdown of the sharp cleavages of the religious communities were within its power.

EDUCATION

In the seventh section education was discussed. Not only were educational opportunities to be guaranteed to all, including Arabs (in Arabic), but the Government assumed responsibility for the promotion of science, letters and arts, the translation of the world's classics into Hebrew, the advancement of pure and applied research, and the establishment of cultural links with Jews everywhere. Sacred learning was specifically included in connection with this international effort.

Free education was to be established and made compulsory by law. Stipends were to be given to worthy students to continue their studies in secondary schools and institutions of higher learning. The minimum curriculum was set forth for primary schools, and this included vocational and agricultural training. This was important because one school system—that of the extremely orthodox Agudat Yisrael—was most deficient in its attention to physical and scientific training and even to the humanities other than sacred literature. Youth movements were also to be supported by the state to the ultimate end of colonization and economic development.

VETERANS' RIGHTS

The eighth section dealt with veterans' rights to former positions, priority in public service, vocational training, special privileges in economic readjustment, and continuation of their education. Disabled veterans were to enjoy still greater priority. The Government also assumed responsibility for supporting families whose mainstay had been killed or disabled in the war.

LABOR

The ninth section set forth labor's "Bill of Rights." The state guaranteed labor's right to organize, to bargain collectively, and to strike. The state was to set minimum wages for different occupations and provide for the mediation of labor disputes. Laborers were assured safe working conditions, security against any and all misfortunes, and vacations. This section also set forth the responsibility of the Government for improving the living standards of Arab workers to the end that there should ultimately be complete equality between Arab and Jew.

Children from ages fifteen to eighteen might work, but evening classes were to be made available to them that they might continue their studies, and their work was to be supervised.

Women were not to engage in occupations that might affect their capacity to become and act as mothers. Maternity leaves were to be compulsory. Night work for mothers was prohibited. Equal pay for males and females doing the same work was guaranteed. The Government was also to provide nurseries for children whose mothers were employed away from home.

A central labor bureau was to provide work for all seeking it, without discrimination as to creed, nationality, party, or sex. Statutes were to so provide.

CIVIL SERVICE

The last section recognized the principle of appointment to civil service by competitive examinations prepared by a non-partisan commission. During the days of the Provisional Government each ministry was staffed principally by persons who were adherents of the political party of the minister in charge.[12] This situation evoked considerable criticism. The fact was, however, that Israel did not have an adequate number of schools to train civil servants.[13]

COMPARISON WITH PROVISIONS OF KOHN DRAFT

How did the Fundamental Principles adopted by the First Kneset compare with those proposed by Dr. Kohn in his draft for a constitution? The deviations may reflect trends that are significant.

Dr. Kohn had provided for the right of any Jew anywhere to immigrate into Israel.[14] However, he made the right "subject to such regulative provisions as may from time to time be enacted" by the legislature. In his comments[15] he noted that by "regulative provisions" he meant only "rules of order." The legislature was not to bar Jewish immigrants because of countries of origin, in-

[12] See H. Lehrman, "The Israelis Learn to Govern Themselves," *Commentary*, VIII, No. 1 (July, 1949), 10, 17, and editorial, "Miflagot u-Peqidut Memshaltit" (Parties and Government Administration), *be-Terem*, 8 Tammuz, 5708: July 15, 1949, p. 6. See also *supra*, p. 80, n. 80, for later developments.

[13] Edwin Samuel, "Israel's Administrative Problems," *Zionist Quarterly*, I, No. 3 (Winter, 1952), 28-34.

[14] *W.H. Proceedings*, Pamphlet II, p. 5.

[15] *Ibid.*, p. 20.

tellectual attainments, or economic conditions. This limitation the Kneset did not specify, but the principle it adopted had at most the status of a statute and was not a constitutional provision. When the principle was finally incorporated in a statute, some limitations were imposed.[16]

In Article 4 of his draft, Dr. Kohn proposed:

> (1) All the inhabitants of Israel shall be subject to one law. The state shall not discriminate against anyone on the grounds of race, religion, language or sex.
>
> (2) All citizens of the State are granted equal civic and political rights. No citizen shall be discriminated against to his disadvantage with regard to public service or promotion therein, on account of his race, religion, language or sex.
>
> (3) No property may be expropriated from any inhabitant of Israel except for public purposes. In all cases of expropriation full compensation, as prescribed by law, shall be paid.[17]

Dr. Kohn drafted this article on the basis of the United Nations General Assembly resolution which required its inclusion in the constitution of Israel. However, a few changes were made by him in the third paragraph. The resolution provided only for the protection of Arab property against confiscation. Dr. Kohn made the rule applicable to all inhabitants. The resolution also called for the assessment by the highest court of the compensation due when private property was taken for a public purpose and for payment in advance of the taking. These requirements Dr. Kohn omitted. It was unreasonable, he argued, to use the highest court for this purpose and it was a needless impediment to state action to insist on payment in advance.[18]

Dr. Milton Konvitz, of Cornell University, raised the objection that Dr. Kohn's provision regarding equality before the law would make it impossible to regulate the conditions under which women were employed and to retain the prevailing family laws "which are premised on the belief that the father or husband

[16] See *infra*, p. 156.

[17] *W.H. Proceedings*, Pamphlet II, pp. 4-5.

[18] *Ibid.*, p. 20.

should be the chief support of the family."[19] For that reason Dr. Konvitz suggested that the word "sex" be omitted. In that way women would be assured the enjoyment of equal civil and political rights and equal economic opportunities.

The difficulty with his proposal was that women in Israel would thus be deprived of a constitutional basis for achieving what they most desire—as equal an opportunity as men enjoy to marry and remarry. By Dr. Kohn's proposal, on the other hand, they would gain this and, in addition, would not lose their special privileges because they were women. Even assuring all citizens in equal measure the protection of the law does not prevent legislators from indulging in classification, and therefore, where required by a reasonable classification, there may be one kind of legislation for males and another for females.

The Kneset did provide special protection for women in the ninth section of its Fundamental Principles, and in the second section it set forth as an ultimate aim complete equality of rights and privileges without discrimination as to sex. It must be remembered, however, that this was not a legal guarantee—it was only a projected end. The legal guarantee came in 1951.[20] The law then approved also afforded women the special protection called for by their own sex.[21] Furthermore, the Kneset guaranteed equal rights only to citizens, not inhabitants, as Dr. Kohn had proposed at least with regard to nonpolitical rights. This may have to wait for the ultimate peace when the entire Arab population will have been integrated into the state. Otherwise, the substance of Dr. Kohn's Article 4 has been adopted by the First Kneset.

In Article 11 of his draft Dr. Kohn provided:[22]

The state of Israel shall seek to settle all international disputes, in

[19] M. Konvitz, "The Bill of Rights in the Draft Constitution for Israel," *The Reconstructionist*, XIV, No. 20 (February 4, 1949), 12-14.

[20] *Sefer ha-Huqim, 5711*, pp. 248-49.

[21] *Ibid.*, sec. 6.

[22] *W.H. Proceedings*, Pamphlet II, p. 6.

which it may be involved, whatever their nature or origin may be, by pacific means. The rules of international law recognized by the nations generally shall form part of the law of Israel.

The United Nations resolution stated that the constitution of Israel should provide for the peaceful adjudication of all international disputes and a prohibition against the use of force or terror. Dr. Kohn felt that a clause in the constitution could only obligate the State to exert every effort for the amicable settlement of controversies.[23] Therefore he incorporated the language of the Kellogg-Briand Pact in the article, instead of the language of the United Nations resolution.

The second sentence of his article was similar to a provision contained in the constitutions of Germany (1919), Estonia, and Eire.[24] Its aim was to compel judges to take judicial notice of international law in all matters before them. The word "nations" implied that the rule of international law—to be recognized—must be one accepted by all the nations. Therefore, if Israel's legislature passed a law denying or modifying that rule, the courts were bound only to recognize the rule established by their legislature, for the rule would then no longer enjoy the approval of all the nations—Israel having excluded itself. Thus Dr. Kohn had reasoned.[25]

This recommendation was not incorporated in the Fundamental Principles. Also omitted were any references to capital or other cruel punishments, the manner of obtaining confessions, imprisonment for debt, the circumstances of lawful detention, *ex post facto* laws,[26] searches and seizures, and the right to privacy—all of which were fully provided for by Dr. Kohn.[27]

Dr. Kohn had also provided for a number of limitations on

[23] *Ibid.*, p. 21. [24] *Ibid.* [25] *Ibid.*

[26] Wahrhaftig tried to have some of these limitations imposed with regard to criminal laws (*Divrei ha-Kneset*, I, 1st Sess., 4th meeting, 33-34). He also wanted soldiers protected by the provisions of the law dealing with courts-martial (*ibid.*, II, 1st Sess., 68th meeting, p. 1357).

[27] *W.H. Proceedings*, Pamphlet II, pp. 7-8.

freedom of expression and freedom to organize. He proposed[28] Articles 16 and 17 as follows:

> ARTICLE 16. Freedom of speech and freedom of opinion in writing or in any other form of expression, are guaranteed. This guarantee shall not apply to publications which are libelous, slanderous or obscene, and not to publications which are designed to stir up racial or religious hatred, or to incite to violence or crime, and not to publications which advocate the suppression of human rights and fundamental freedoms, or the betrayal of the democratic system of government, and not to publications which reveal secrets of national defence. The institution of preventive censorship shall be unlawful save in time of war or national emergency by specific legislative authorization whose execution shall be under continuous supervision of the Chamber of Deputies.
>
> ARTICLE 17. Citizens of Israel shall have the right to assemble peaceably and without arms and to form associations, subject to such regulative provisions which the laws of the state will prescribe. Such enactments shall contain no discrimination on grounds of race, religion, language or political belief.
>
> This guarantee shall not apply to assemblies or associations aiming at the suppression of human rights and fundamental freedoms or the betrayal of the democratic form of government.

The Fundamental Principles of the First Kneset conditioned these freedoms upon the following: "Due regard for the security of the state, its freedom and independence, as well as respect for private rights." This limitation, unfortunately, is very broad. It almost negates the right altogether.

Did the existence of an emergency justify regulations like those of September 20, 1948, which followed the assassination of Bernadotte, and which prohibited terrorist activity?[29] In a criminal prosecution under the regulation, an organization was presumptively terrorist by Government declaration alone. Proof that an individual was a member of a terrorist organization at any

[28] *Ibid.*, p. 8.

[29] See *M.H.H. Proceedings*, 19th meeting, pp. 31-34; *'Iton Rishmi*, No. 22, Supp. 2, September 20, 1948, pp. 145-48.

time after May 14, 1948 was presumptive evidence that he was still such. As a matter of fact, the property of a terrorist organization was forfeited even if acquired before the publication of the regulation.

The Kneset, however, expanded upon Dr. Kohn's proposals on social and economic rights. The state assumed complete responsibility for the welfare of its citizens. The rights were not only hortatory. The executive authority was made responsible for their implementation.

ISRAEL A "POSITIVE STATE"

Israel was committed to the philosophy of the "positive state."[30] Governmental activity was to penetrate into almost every field of human endeavor. One wonders, therefore, all the more that so few fears were expressed by its subjects that it might ultimately become totalitarian. Can it be that this type of alarm prevails only in countries where the rich are numerous and can induce it? Or is it the fact that most Israelis are reconciled to the "ingathering of exiles" and understand that to fulfill this program the state must act on many fronts?

Constitution makers cannot forever ignore the threat to personal freedom from a welfare state whose legislation has no restraints whatever from either an oral or written constitution.

[30] W. Ebenstein, *Introduction to Political Philosophy* (New York, 1952), p. 5.

CHAPTER VII

Constitutional Patterns of the First Kneset

ORGANIZATION OF THE STATE AND ITS LEGISLATIVE PROCESS

The First Kneset approved not only the Transition Law and the Fundamental Principles, which have great constitutional significance, but fashioned the constitutional pattern that was likely to continue for a long time to come.

As has already been indicated, it established a parliamentary form of government. The Kneset was the legislative authority. It also elected the president. From its membership the president designated the person to organize the cabinet or Government, which exercised executive power. The judiciary, in turn, was organized under, and supervised by, the Ministry of Justice, which because of its significant role in both lawmaking and law enforcement was in an excellent position to perform significant tasks of coordination.

Statutes were usually proposed by the Government, though members of the Kneset had the right to propose them as well.[1] The ministry concerned with the statute prepared the bill and submitted it to the Government for approval after it had been examined by the Ministry of Justice from the point of view of legislative draftsmanship. The draft was then delivered to the presiding officer of the Kneset. Copies of the proposed statute were placed in the portfolio of every member of the Kneset at least forty-eight hours in advance of the general debate or "first

[1] Legislative procedure is discussed in A. Zidon, *ha-Kneset* (Tel Aviv, 5710), pp. 111-14.

reading." The discussion was opened by the interested minister or committee chairman, who sometimes read parts of the bill aloud with comments. Members of the Kneset participated in the debate, following which the bill was either referred to the appropriate committee, returned to the Government, or dropped from the agenda. In the debate within the committee to which the bill was referred the interested minister participated as well as a representative of the Ministry of Justice. By majority vote within the committee the bill was usually redrafted, but proposed amendments which were not approved by a majority were nonetheless included in the committee's report to the Kneset. Twenty-four hours before the second reading every member of the Kneset received a copy of the proposed statute as approved by the committee's majority and a copy of amendments proposed but not approved. The committee's chairman or a member of the committee's majority made the second reading, paragraph by paragraph, with comments. Dissenters within the committee then discussed their amendments or opposition. The Kneset voted on each paragraph after the debate thereon. The last reading, which might take place at the same meeting or at a subsequent one, was made by the Kneset chairman, and a vote taken on the bill as a whole.

That the Government usually took the initiative in legislation, however, did not mean that the Kneset gave its perfunctory approval to all proposed legislation. On the other hand, as a result of the debates within the Kneset, and particularly within the committees to which the bills were referred, proposed bills were often rewritten with radical changes. For example, the Government's proposed Compulsory Education Law[2] was so rewritten that it became almost twice as large as the original proposal.[3] The bill as finally passed added compulsory education for adolescents who had no primary school education;[4] it stated the

[2] *Reshumot, Haza'ot Hok*, No. 16, June 11, 1949, pp. 163-67.
[3] *Sefer ha-Huqim, 5709*, pp. 287-94. [4] *Ibid.*, p. 289.

responsibility of employers[5] as well as parents of minors to the children affected by the law, and the ultimate responsibility of the state[6] as distinguished from joint responsibility with municipal or local school boards, for the enforcement of the law. Similarly the Kneset committee made changes in the Government's proposed Law of Return.[7] The Government had proposed that the right of immigration into Israel be denied anyone who had acted against the interests of the Jewish people or the Jewish state. The Kneset committee eliminated the words "against the Jewish state," and the Kneset approved the change.[8] The Head of the Government, who participated in the debate in the Kneset, even expressed his criticism of one change which the committee had made in the proposed bill.[9]

In addition to statutes, the Kneset considered reports by ministers of the Government on all foreign and domestic affairs. Following each of these reports there usually was a general debate, after which the reporting minister often offered rebuttal or summation. The Kneset's conclusions were incorporated in resolutions. The procedure with regard to questions and answers was the same as in the State Council of the Provisional Government.[10] However, the debates on the ministers' reports and answers to questions constituted another effective means by which the Kneset influenced and guided the Government.

The Government, nonetheless, enjoyed the dominant position in the process of legislation. Whether the situation could be regarded as "cabinet dictatorship"[11] is difficult to say. In England, a bill proposed by a private member of the House of Commons occasionally becomes law, though the mortality of such bills is

[5] *Ibid.*
[6] *Ibid.*, p. 292.
[7] *Reshumot, Haza'ot Hok*, No. 48, June 27, 1950, p. 189.
[8] *Sefer ha-Huqim, 5710*, p. 159.
[9] *Divrei ha-Kneset*, VI, 2d Sess. 162nd Meeting, 2099.
[10] See *supra*, p. 55.
[11] F. A. Ogg, *European Government and Politics* (New York, 3d ed., 1939), p. 259.

high.[12] In Israel, during the period of the First Kneset, not one such bill was approved. As a matter of fact, Ada Maimon (Member of the Kneset) proposed a law nullifying child marriages. Because of the opposition of the Religious Bloc, the Government did not support the measure. Instead it submitted its own proposal to punish the persons responsible for child marriages, without voiding the marriages. In this form the measure became law.[13]

The dominant position of the Government in legislation not only lessens the importance of the Kneset but also places a heavy burden on the ministers. In a two party system, the ministry interested in a bill prepares it and the other ministries are confident that it expresses cabinet policy. With many parties in the Government, each minister senses not only that he is responsible for his particular executive department but that he must safeguard his party's interests in the proposals of ministries headed by members of parties other than his own. Party conflict and suspicion are so intense that "no one is willing to trust anyone else with an important political or even administrative undertaking. . . . Ministers rush from one committee to another."[14] They are, therefore, overworked.

The political party heads share the same concern in Kneset committees. Each wants to protect his party and its point of view. And because the members of the Kneset really represent their parties rather than constituents in a particular area, their proposals to amend bills and even their inquiries of ministers more often reflect a desire to advance a party objective than the requirements of one citizen or another.

The liberty of action enjoyed by an ordinary congressman in the United States House of Representatives is decidedly greater than that of a member of the Kneset. Whether or not the latter would participate in a debate was decided in Israel by the party

[12] *Ibid.*, p. 230. [13] See *infra*, p. 134.

[14] Edwin Samuel, "Israel's Administrative Problems," Zionist Quarterly, I, No. 3, 30.

head,[15] and rarely did one have permission to oppose a measure sponsored by the party leaders. Many of these evils, however, cannot be eliminated until political parties are fewer in number.

RELATIONSHIP BETWEEN THE GOVERNMENT AND THE KNESET ON BUDGET AND TREATIES

On December 26, 1949,[16] the Kneset began its debate on the ratification of the Convention for the Prevention and Punishment of the Crime of Genocide adopted by the United Nations General Assembly. The Convention was approved two days later,[17] and the Minister of Justice made some significant comments.[18] He indicated, without citing authority or being challenged,[19] that the Government could ratify treaties without consulting the Kneset. However, without Kneset confirmation the treaties would not become a part of the domestic law.[20] With the Kneset's confirmation, the Genocide Convention has come to be regarded in Israel as one of the few fundamental laws of the new state.[21]

With regard to the budget, each ministry submitted its proposed annual budget to the Ministry of Finance, which, after making whatever changes it considered necessary, presented the combined budget to the cabinet.[22] After approval by the Government the budget was sent to the Kneset with a statement of estimated revenues and a breakdown of expenditures.[23]

The Minister of Finance opened the Kneset debate on the

[15] See *infra*, p. 171.

[16] *Divrei ha-Kneset*, III, 2d Sess., 98th Meeting, 313-24.

[17] *Ibid.*, p. 345. [18] *Ibid.*, p. 323.

[19] The acceptance of the American loan in 1948 was done with the approval of the Mo'ezat ha-Medinah ha-Zemanit, and not by the Provisional Government alone. During the debate on the Constitution, Beigin of Herut did raise the point. He objected to the ratification of treaties by the Government alone without Kneset approval in advance (*Divrei ha-Kneset*, IV, 2d Sess., 113th meeting, 736). See also Wahrhaftig's view, *ibid.*, 111th meeting, 700.

[20] The law implementing the treaty in Israel was passed (*Sefer ha-Huqim, 5710*, pp. 137-38).

[21] *Government Yearbook, 5711*, p. 62.

[22] Zidon, *ha-Kneset*, p. 156. [23] *Ibid.*

budget, which usually included an exhaustive discussion of both the economic and fiscal policies of the Government.[24] The finance committee also conducted an extensive debate which was usually repeated when it reported the budget out of committee, with majority and minority views, together with a budget law.[25]

The debates afforded members of the Kneset with an opportunity to criticize the work of individual ministries and the economic, political, religious, and social program of the Government. That was probably why no annual budget was ever approved by the beginning of the fiscal period,[26] and interim budgets had to be approved for periods ranging from one to three months.[27] The vote in the Kneset was taken on each appropriation—which was usually for a ministry or department.

If a ministry subsequently wanted to transfer an appropriation from one purpose to another it might have done so with the approval of the Ministry of Finance and/or the Kneset committee on finance.[28] The Minister of Finance could also increase the appropriation to a ministry by using the reserves.[29] Military appropriations, however, were made by the Finance Committee on the recommendation of the Government,[30] though partial appropriations were included in the general budget.[31]

It can be said that the power of the purse in Israel passed to the Government. The debates in the Kneset on sundry budgets were nothing more than opportunities for the opposition to voice grievances and bring the political policy of the Government under critical review. There was no dispassionate, straightforward, constructive financial criticism, though this may have been forth-

[24] *Ibid.* [25] *Ibid.*

[26] *Government Yearbook, 5711*, p. 62, and *Sefer ha-Huqim, 5709*, p. 201.

[27] The Budget Law for the fiscal year April 1, 1949 to March 31, 1950, was first debated on August 31, 1949. The Finance Committee's report was approved without a single amendment (*Divrei ha-Kneset*, II, 1st Sess., 74th meeting, 1508).

[28] *Sefer ha-Huqim, 5709*, p. 202, sec. 8. [29] *Ibid.*, sec. 5.

[30] *Ibid.*, sec. 6, and Zidon, *ha-Kneset*, p. 156. [31] *Ibid.*, p. 158.

coming within the Kneset committee. The primary responsibility for preventing extravagance, therefore, rested with the Government. Cabinet control has overreached into this area as well.

ARAB PARTICIPATION

It is estimated that 80 percent of the Arab population of that part of Palestine which was allocated to the Jewish state fled during the war.[32] After the conclusion of the armistice with Jordan many returned, and by 1951 there were about 170,000 in Israel.[33] These included Muslims (119,000), Christians (35,-000), and Druzes (15,000).[34] In the First Kneset, however, only three served as members. One was elected on the Communist Party List, and two were elected on the Democratic List of Nazareth, a list sponsored by Mapai.

The political integration of the non-Jewish population varied. The Druzes and the Circassians not only welcomed the establishment of the Jewish state but even volunteered to fight in its defense. Relations between them and the Jewish authorities were friendly. Most of the Arabs, however, were subject to military government during the term of the First Kneset.[35] As a result, young men of military age were interned, entire Arab villages were moved away from the borders, and urban residents were moved into areas of "concentration" where they could be more easily watched. Thus, though by the Kneset's Fundamental Principles they were guaranteed the privileges of citizenship, the process of political integration continued to be slow.

The Arab members of the Kneset sat on several parliamentary committees, participated in Kneset debates, and enjoyed all the

[32] M. Assaf, "The Non-Jewish Population of Israel," *Israel,* January, 1950, p. 27.

[33] D. R. Elston, "Arabs in Israel," *Israel and Middle East,* III, No. 1-2 (January-March, 1951), 21, and *Government Yearbook, 5712,* p. 344.

[34] *Ibid.*

[35] Assaf, "Non-Jewish Population," *Israel,* p. 28, and Elston, "Arabs in Israel," *Israel and Middle East,* p. 22.

rights and privileges of Kneset members. They addressed the Kneset in Arabic. All the proceedings were translated for them instantly by an official translator who communicated with them via earphones attached to their seats—as in the United Nations.[36] The manner in which the Arab population as a whole was affected by sundry constitutional issues and patterns is discussed elsewhere in this study.

PROCEDURE IN THE KNESET

The First Kneset elected two vice-chairmen instead of three as the State Council had.[37] The standing committees were reduced in number to nine,[38] as follows:

> Committee of the Kneset: concerned with standing orders and rules of Kneset procedure; the composition of all committees; referrals to them; eligibility of, and complaints against, members of the Kneset; their salaries; petitions; and all other matters not related to the work of, or assigned to, other committees.
>
> Committee on Finance: budget, taxes and imposts, loans, coinage, banks, stamps, income and expenditures of the state, franchises, state-owned property, alien property, and liaison with the Comptroller General.
>
> Committee on the Economy: trade and industry, rationing and supply, agriculture and fisheries, communications, cooperatives, and regulation and balancing of the economy.
>
> Committee on Foreign Affairs and Security.
>
> Committee on Interior: local government and domestic policy, immigration, newspapers and publications, citizenship, and the building of cities.[39]
>
> Committee on Constitution, Law, and Justice.
>
> Committee on Public Services: health, social welfare, and benefits to disabled veterans.
>
> Committee on Education and Culture: science, art, radio transmission, cinema, and physical culture.

[36] *Government Yearbook, 5711*, p. 64.
[37] *Divrei ha-Kneset*, I, 1st Sess., 1st meeting, 12.
[38] *Ibid.*, 16th meeting, p. 197.
[39] On July 13, 1949, there was added the organization of the religious communities. *Ibid.*, II, 1st Sess., 55th meeting, 1008.

Committee on Labor: reconstruction, housing, rehabilitation of veterans, and social security.

The parties in opposition to the coalition Government hoped to increase the number of the committees so that there would be one committee for each ministry.[40] In that way the legislature might exercise greater control over the executive. To this the Head of the Government objected.[41] The responsibility of the executive was a collective one as set forth in the Fundamental Principles. Individual ministers were not to be accountable to particular committees of the Kneset.[42]

The parties were represented in the committees in proportion to their strength in the Kneset. Two of the committees—those on Kneset and Constitution, Law, and Justice—had twenty-three members, while the remainder had only fifteen.

Every party represented in the Kneset could appoint one of its members to consultative status on one of the two larger committees. Interparty agreements might also be made, with the approval of the Committee of the Kneset, as to how they would divide their representation on these two committees.[43] The distribution of committe seats to the parties was considered fair by all except the Communist party, which protested.[44]

A parliamentary system of standing committees, such as England and the United States have, usually helps to develop more expertness on the part of committee members in one major subject of legislation. However, Israel failed to gain full advantage of this opportunity. Again because of party suspicion and hostility, each party felt that it must carefully protect its interests in all the committees. But most of the parties did not have a

[40] *Ibid.*, I, 1st Sess., 16th meeting, 212. [41] *Ibid.*, 218-220.

[42] "Several Israel Cabinet Ministers have tried to avoid consulting their respective parliamentary committees on routine matters and even on matters of greater importance . . . Yet, on the whole, the parliamentary committees have retained their power, although they do allow the ministers a certain amount of discretion" (E. Laserson, "How is Israel Governed," *New Palestine*, May, 1950, p. 9).

[43] *Divrei ha-Kneset*, I, 1st Sess., 17th meeting, 236. [44] *Ibid.*

PARTY REPRESENTATION IN THE STANDING COMMITTEES OF THE FIRST KNESET[a]
JULY, 1949

Party	*Constitution, Law, and Justice*	*Kneset*	*Foreign Affairs and Security*	*Public Services*	*Labor*	*Education and Culture*	*Economy*	*Finance*	*Interior*
Mapai	8	8	7[b]	7	5[b]	6	6	5	5
Mapam	4[b]	4	2	2	3	2	2[b]	3	2
Religious Bloc	3	3	2	2	2	2	2	2[b]	2[b]
Herut	3	3	2	2[b]	1	2	2	2	1
General Zionists	1	1	1	1	1	1[b]	1	1	1
Progressives	1	1[b]	1		1		1	1	1
Sephardim	1	1			1			1	
Israeli Communists	1	1					1		1
Democrats of Nazareth	1	1							1
WIZO						1			
Fighters									1
Yemenites					1				
Hebrew Communists				1					
Total	23	23	15	15	15	15	15	15	15

[a] Zidon, *ha-Kneset*, p. 92. [b] Indicates chairmanship of committee.

sufficient number of representatives to name one to each committee, even if permitted to do so. There were 151 committee seats to be assigned to 120 persons. Formal fairness in the assignments, therefore, was not enough. The smaller parties wanted their few spokesmen to be virtually omnipresent. And they not only had no chance to develop expertness in a particular phase but could hardly constitute a constructively critical force in legislation.

Within the Kneset, the total time allotted for debate was usually determined by the Kneset's presidium, or by the committee on the Kneset, or the Kneset itself.[45] It was then distributed among members of the Kneset in proportion to party strength. Each party then divided its total time among the speakers it designated to participate in the debate. Parties with only one member in the Kneset were each given an additional five minutes.[46]

The debate was privileged, and only during a state of emergency could the Kneset chairman rule any comment unpublishable for reasons of security.[47]

From rulings of the Kneset chairman on the interpretation of rules or precedents a member could appeal to a rulings committee consisting of the Kneset chairman, his two deputies ex officio, and four members of the Kneset chosen by the Committee on the Kneset.[48]

ORGANIZATION OF THE GOVERNMENT

During the period of the First Kneset the ministers were selected only from the parties who joined in the coalition, whereas all the major parties had had portfolios in the Provisional Government. The Head of the Government submitted a slate of twelve ministers[49] instead of thirteen as had the Provisional

[45] Zidon, *ha-Kneset*, pp. 112, 181-82, and *Government Yearbook, 5711*, p. 63.

[46] *Ibid.* [47] *Ibid.* [48] *Ibid.*

[49] *Divrei ha-Kneset*, I, 1st Sess., 7th meeting, 54.

Government. Four portfolios were held in reserve in the hope that additional parties would join the coalition.[50]

The departments (Misradim), many of which had been instituded by the Provisional Government, usually comprised a number of divisions (Agafim) and sections (Mahlaqot). There was, however, no uniform pattern of organization. A director general usually served under the minister, and the former in turn might have had under him a number of directors heading different departments. Usually there were so many of these departments under one director general that he had to spend most of his time interviewing his immediate associates, with little opportunity to receive the public, inspect suboffices, or do his own work.[51] This came about largely because individuals who were to head divisions would use party influence to elevate themselves to positions as department heads and thus become accountable directly to the Director General. The divisions and sections, in turn, functioned under division and section heads, respectively. The lowest executive appointment in the Israeli administration was a section head. The sections usually had branches in major cities. Yet policies were determined only by the central office. The branch offices could do nothing but file or forward, a situation it was hoped would be bettered when an adequate number of civil servants had been trained.

The Government has fully publicized the work of all the departments in three Yearbooks, published for each of the years 5710, 5711, and 5712 (1949–50, 1950–51 and 1951–52).[52] An examination of this material reveals the extent to which the ministries were concerned with every kind of development conceivable—economic, political, social, cultural, legal, religious,

[50] These portfolios were Commerce and Industry, Health, Agriculture, and Minorities (*ibid.*, 55).

[51] Samuel, "Administrative Problems," *Zionist Quarterly*, p. 33.

[52] *Shenaton ha-Memshalah, 5710*, pp. 15-187; *Government Yearbook, 5711*, pp. 72-216, and *Government Yearbook, 5712*, pp. 22-155. See also G. De Gaury, *The New State of Israel* (New York, 1952).

military. From a constitutional point of view, however, it is of interest that Israel has virtually no administrative law courts. Persons aggrieved by administrative rulings, therefore, had to resort to the established courts or seek intercession in their behalf by some party leader.

The ministries also promulgated administrative regulations[53] which were published in the *Reshumot*. However, these were also officially presented to the Kneset and members of the Kneset occasionally raised issues with regard to them.[54] The issues thus raised were referred to the appropriate committees of the Kneset, which investigated and reported.

In England there are in the larger departments one or two parliamentary undersecretaries and a secretary, all of whom share the burden of expounding departmental policy in the legislature, serving on committees, and supervising operations. In Israel, in most cases, all of this was done by one man. Of great assistance to the ministers, however, was the cabinet secretariat, patterned after England's. Zev Sharef, Secretary to the Government and senior civil servant, also had the duties of Civil Service Commissioner. He coordinated the work of the different departments even as he provided them with personnel.

THE PRESIDENT AND THE COMPTROLLER

Chaim Weizmann was elected president of the First Kneset on February 16, 1949.[55] His limited functions have already been described, but his powers and prerogatives were subsequently enlarged to the extent of permitting him to appoint the comptroller upon the nomination of the Committee on the Kneset.[56]

The law creating this office was much broader than the original proposal contained in Article 69 of Dr. Kohn's draft for a constitution, which read as follows:

[53] Zidon, *ha-Kneset*, p. 120.
[54] E.g., *Divrei ha-Kneset*, IV, 2d Sess., 109th meeting, 637-38.
[55] *Divrei ha-Kneset*, I, 1st Sess., 5th meeting, 49.
[56] *Sefer ha-Huqim, 5709*, p. 33.

There shall be appointed a comptroller and auditor general to review, on behalf of the state, all payments and to examine all accounts of monies administered by or under the authority of the Chamber of Deputies. The comptroller and auditor general shall not be a member of the Chamber of Deputies and shall not be permitted to hold other office or position of emolument. The manner of his appointment, the term of his office, and the conditions of his work, shall be fixed by law.[57]

Dr. Kohn drafted this article in accordance with the British practice. In mose countries of continental Europe, he indicated, the functions of comptroller and auditor general were performed by committees comprising a number of civil servants.[58]

Instead of this one article, however, Professor Vitta had proposed two articles consisting of seven sections.[59] He felt that to provide for only one independent agency in addition to the legislative and executive authorities was not enough. There should be at least a Judicial Council to advise the Government on all legislative and administrative matters. This council might also function as the highest tribunal in matters of administrative law. He would have called this organ the "Council of State"[60] and a second organ the "Council of the Comptroller."[61]

[57] *W.H. Proceedings*, Pamphlet II, p. 13.

[58] *Ibid.*, p. 34.

[59] *Ibid.*, Pamphlet V, pp. 49-56.

[60] *Ibid.*, pp. 24-26. For Israel, Professor Vitta recommended such a council consisting of between six and nine members, appointed by the president on the joint recommendation of the Ministers of Interior and Justice, after consultation with the Government. The appointees should be outstanding lawyers, professors of law, and experienced civil servants. One of the high officials shall be its chairman that he may be invited to attend meetings of the cabinet in an advisory capacity. The Council shall advise on all important administrative acts of the Government and all proposed acts, orders, regulations and other matters of a legislative character. To assign to this Council appellate jurisdiction in matters of administrative law could only be done when and if it were decided that there will be a special system of administrative law courts.

[61] *Ibid.*, pp. 26-27. With regard to the office of comptroller and auditor general, Professor Vitta called attention to the practices prevailing in other countries. For Israel he recommended the following:

1 (a) A council of the comptroller, directly connected with the Cham-

The law approved by the Kneset[62] comprised some of the recommendations of both Kohn and Vitta. The comptroller was to make recommendations for legislation, but he had no powers comparable to those of Vitta's projected Council of State. However, the comptroller did more than simply approve disbursements. He was also the "efficiency expert" for all national and municipal undertakings, for example, postal and communication services, alien and refugee property, and so forth. For this reason he had deputies in almost all the ministries and departments.

Though he was appointed by the president upon the nomination of the committee of the Kneset, he rendered his reports and made his recommendations to the Finance Committee of the Kneset. He was accountable only to the Kneset, which could have removed him by a vote of two-thirds of the members voting. His term expired four months after the expiration of the term of the Kneset whose committee had nominated him.

The office of comptroller and auditor general had a major re-

---

ber of Deputies, shall assist the Chamber in supervising the accounts and expenditures of the state.

(b) The council shall consist of a chairman and a number of members who will be chosen by the Chamber of Deputies from a list of persons nominated by the Council of State. The list shall consist of at least twice as many names as there are vacancies to be filled.

(c) The council, whose organization and powers shall be fixed by law, shall be established on the principle that its members are independent, and can only be removed by a vote of two thirds of the Deputies.

2 (a) This council shall examine the accounts of the Government and advise the Chamber whether or not to approve the Government's expenditures.

(b) The Chamber can authorize this council to examine all institutions, funds and departments, which the Government conducts, and also all in which the Government participates.

(c) All Government notes, which are Government obligations, shall bear the counter-signature of the chairman of this council.

(d) The fiscal management of cities, with populations of 20,000 or over shall be under the supervision of this council, which will advise the Government on the results of its inspection. When requested by the Government for cause, the council shall also supervise the fiscal affairs of cities and municipal councils with populations less than 20,000.

[62] *Sefer ha-Huqim, 5709,* pp. 33-36, and Zidon, *ha-Kneset,* pp. 147-48.

sponsibility during the period of the First Kneset. To say the least, the financial methods of those civil servants whom the Government had acquired from the Jewish Agency and Wa'ad Leumi were "highly optimistic and unconventional."[63] To change this characteristic was the aim of the new office.

[63] Samuel, "Administrative Problems," *Zionist Quarterly*, p. 31.

CHAPTER VIII

Toward a Written Constitution

On the first anniversary of its convening, the Kneset opened debate on the issue of a written constitution.[1] The chairman of the Committee on Constitution, Law, and Justice, Nahum Nir-Raffalkes, was the first speaker, and he favored an affirmative resolution of the problem. As a member of Mapam—a party in opposition to the coalition government—he did not hesitate to criticize the Government for its decision to table the matter.[2] Subsequently, he was supported by spokesmen of other parties in the opposition, Menahem Beigin of Herut,[3] Ya'aqov Gil of the General Zionists,[4] and Meir Vilner of the Communists[5] as well as by other members of his own party.[6] The only party represented in the coalition Government which took the same stand was the Progressive Party,[7] but members of Mapai as individuals expressed concurring views.[8] The parties whose spokesmen were virtually unanimous in opposition to a written constitution were the religious parties in the United Religious Bloc.[9]

The debate was held on nine different days between February 1 and June 13, 1950, when a resolution was finally approved.[10] None of the usual limitations on debate in the Kneset was invoked.

[1] *Divrei ha-Kneset*, IV, 2d Sess., 112th meeting, 714.
[2] *Ibid.*, 715.
[3] *Ibid.*, 113th meeting, 736.
[4] *Ibid.*, 745.
[5] *Ibid.*, 115th meeting, 800.
[6] *Ibid.*, 113th meeting, 733.
[7] *Ibid.*, 115th meeting, 776.
[8] *Ibid.*, 113th meeting, 741.
[9] *Ibid.*, 729.
[10] *Ibid.*, V, 2d Sess., 151st meeting, 1722.

SUMMARY OF ARGUMENTS FOR

The proponents of a written constitution argued as follows:

Israel's Proclamation of Independence[11] called for it, as did the United Nations General Assembly resolution.[12] In addition, when Israelis voted for delegates to the Constituent Assembly they understood that it was to the end that a written constitution would be drafted. Good faith required that they should not be disappointed.[13]

Israel required a charter of government that would define the powers of the legislative, executive and judicial authorities. It was pointed out that the existence of the Kneset itself was precarious, for it might be dissolved by the Government under existing emergency legislation, and after such a dissolution the Government could indefinitely decline to call an election.[14]

A written constitution would prevent the usurpation of power by any one branch of the Government. That England does not require a written constitution is insignificant. England has a democratic tradition established over a period of centuries, and her citizens understand and respect it while Israel is a new state whose democratic character must be firmly secured in a brief interval of time.[15]

A written constitution would better guarantee fundamental freedoms[16] and human rights, particularly equality of the sexes and the equality of heretics.[17] Israel, it was said, suffered too many instances of unlawful searches and censorship.[18] On the basis of a written constitution a citizen could more readily assert and defend his rights against the Government.[19]

A written constitution would have great educational value;[20] it could be studied by children in the schools more readily than

[11] *Mo'ezat ha-'Am, Proceedings*, 4th meeting, p. 25.

[12] *Supra*, p. 11.

[13] See *supra*, p. 62, as to whether failure to draft a written constitution was a surprise to the electors.

[14] *Divrei ha-Kneset*, IV, 2d Sess., 112th meeting, 717.

[15] *Ibid.*, 113th meeting, 746.

[16] *Ibid.*, 737.

[17] *Ibid.*, 736, and 117th meeting, 824.

[18] *Ibid.*, 113th meeting, 737.

[19] *Ibid.*, 745.

[20] *Ibid.*, 742.

an oral constitution, and it would help immigrants the more easily to become familiar with the nature of their new state. It would expedite their re-education and reorientation.[21]

Furthermore, a written constitution would be an affirmation to all the nations of the earth that Israel is a stable, sovereign, democratic state.[22] Within Israel it would become the symbol of national unity.

The proponents of a written constitution generally favored one that could be amended easily.[23] One speaker even mentioned specifically that dread of a tribunal similar to the United States Supreme Court should not deter Israel from having a written charter of government. Israel could adopt another method for the adjudication of constitutional issues.[24]

SUMMARY OF ARGUMENTS AGAINST

Opposition to a written constitution came principally from representatives of the religious parties and the Head of the Government, David Ben Gurion. As already indicated,[25] he altered his stand on the issue. And most of the religious parties were also guilty of a reversal of position. Within the Committee on the Constitution of the State Council of the Provisional Government only the spokesman of the Agudat Yisrael expressed the hope that the Torah would be Israel's constitution.[26] Wahrhaftig, the Committee's chairman and spokesman for Mizrahi and ha-Po'el ha-Mizrahi, saw no conflict between his religious view and a projected written charter of government. For his change of heart he was criticized in the Kneset by Nir-Raffalkes.[27] Wahrhaftig and his colleagues in the United Religious Bloc had yielded to the pressure of the rabbinic leaders of the Agudat Yisrael.[28] One ha-Po'el ha-Mizrahi leader subsequently criticized this deference

[21] *Ibid.*, 734.
[22] *Ibid.*, 745.
[23] *Ibid.*, 115th meeting, 783.
[24] *Ibid.*, 112th meeting, 717.
[25] *Supra*, p. 16.
[26] *Supra*, p. 46.
[27] *Divrei ha-Kneset*, IV, 2d Sess., 112th meeting, 716.
[28] Editorials, *ha-Arez*, XXXII, No. 9366, June 7, 1950, 1, and No. 9371, June 13, 1950, 2.

to Agudat Yisrael and revealed that several of his party's spokesmen favored a written constitution.[29] In the Kneset debate, however, opposition to a written constitution was based upon the following arguments:

Israel's constitution should be a bridge between the Jewish past and the Jewish future. It should reflect the Jewish "volksgeist."[30] Simply to include in it the platitudes with which modern constitutions abound would be useless. In due time the historic process itself would cause the most desirable forms of the state to evolve.[31]

The drafting of a constitution should await the fulfillment of the "Ingathering of Exiles," for only a small percentage of the Jewish people now resides in Israel and a constitution ought to reflect the will of all rather than the will of only a few.[32]

The Proclamation of Independence was not legally binding on the first democratically elected Kneset so that it had to approve a written constitution. Moreover, the courts had already ruled that the Proclamation had no legal significance.[33] Furthermore, even before the elections to the Constituent Assembly the electorate knew that there was doubt in the minds of many of the candidates regarding the wisdom of immediately adopting a constitution.

The drafting of even the preamble to a written constitution would only aggravate interparty bitterness and hostility when Israel desperately needed greater national unity.[34]

It was sufficient to have "fundamental laws" like the Transi-

[29] M. Una, "mi-Saviv ha-Kneset," *Netiva*, 26th year, No. X, pp. 2-4.

[30] See I. Stein, "Why Is The Israeli Coalition Government Against A Constitution," *Undzer Weg*, 25th year, No. 2 (January 15, 1950), pp. 6-7. The author criticizes the idea of "volksgeist" as affecting a constitution. He claims that Ben Gurion cannot possibly subscribe to such a view. Ben Gurion's opposition is based solely on expediency—his desire to retain the coalition. The author points to the need of a constitution to limit government. Query—is that a Marxist view?

[31] *Divrei ha-Kneset*, IV, 2d Sess., 113th meeting, 732.

[32] This argument was referred to in Nir-Raffalkes's speech (*ibid.*, 112th meeting, 717-18). It was also mentioned by Ben Gurion (*ibid.*, 117th meeting, 819).

[33] *Ibid.*, 113th meeting, 729.

[34] *Ibid.*, 117th meeting, 812.

tion Law. Fundamental laws are more readily amended than a written constitution[35] and those that Israel already had, together with the Jewish legal and ethical tradition, might be regarded as its oral constitution.[36]

With this last argument some members of Mapai agreed.[37] The Kneset had already approved of fundamental principles which were the equivalent of a bill of rights, and the Transition Law provided for the basic structure of the government. More of such laws were required and in due time a written constitution would have emerged. It was argued that to provide for more than fundamental principles at the moment—without waiting for greater experience with regard to their implementation—would be unfortunate. Even the United States had allowed eleven years to elapse between its Declaration of Independence and the writing of its federal constitution.[38] The Head of the Government was generally opposed to the granting of privileged status to any law and that, he felt, would be the effect of a written constitution.[39] The people cannot readily amend privileged laws and thus a written constitution which enjoys privileged status is in effect a negation of democracy. He did not concur, however, in the view that the religious tradition of the Jewish people was hostile to the drafting of a constitution with a secularist tone. As a matter of fact, such a secularist constitution, he argued, would be most consonant with the tradition.[40] Even the prophet Samuel yielded to popular pressure for a king.

The debate, however, yielded more than arguments pro and con. It helped to shed light upon the philosophy and the strategy of the political parties and the personal hostility between a number of their leaders.

Mapai did not exercise party discipline over its members and did not insist on support of the views of the Head of the Govern-

[35] *Ibid.*, 113th meeting, 728.
[36] *Ibid.*, 730.
[37] *Ibid.*, 725-28.
[38] *Ibid.*, 727.
[39] *Ibid.*, 117th meeting, 818.
[40] *Ibid.*, 815.

ment. David Bar-Rav-Hai did support him.[41] He argued that the fundamental principles set forth in the Proclamation of Independence were already a constitution. Israel required nothing loftier. What Israel did require were laws to implement these principles and to enact such laws would take time and experience. For example, the right to work was conceded. However, to so order the economy that the right will be fulfilled for everyone could not be done hastily. He suggested, therefore, that the Committee on the Constitution continue its work on laws which would implement the principles of freedom and equality to which they were all committed, and certainly within a generation a constitution would emerge.

Ben Zion Dinaburg, of Mapai, on the other hand, disagreed[42] with the Head of the Government. He did not see any evil in a law that could not be amended as easily as other laws. To expect a constitution to emerge from a series of laws was to place the cart before the horse. Rather should the laws reflect and implement the constitutional principles. Furthermore, a written constitution would have great educational value. The position of Agudat Yisrael that the Torah should be Israel's constitution he regarded as absurd.

This difference of opinion between members of Mapai is further evidence of the nondoctrinaire character of the party.

Members of Mapam, on the other hand, were unanimous in their opposition to the view of the Head of the Government. Meir Ya'ari[43] accused Mapai of conspiring with the Religious Bloc against a written constitution. This alliance had often been the butt of Mapam criticism. During the course of his speech he attacked the Herut party as well, and as happened often during the debate, his speech was interrupted by incriminations and recriminations from members of the party attacked. Joseph Lamm of Mapai spoke[44] of the unfitness of Herut and Mapam represen-

[41] *Ibid.*, 113th meeting, 725-28.
[42] *Ibid.*, 741-43.
[43] *Ibid.*, 115th meeting, 766-70.
[44] *Ibid.*, 116th meeting, 796-800.

tatives to draft a democratic constitution. Menahem Beigin of Herut, in his speech favoring a written constitution, had anticipated[45] this *ad hominem* attack. After all, his party had defied the rule of law under the mandatory and now it was espousing the cause of a strict legal order under a constitution. He pointed to the difference between British rule and an Israeli state. The former was slavery but the latter required laws of freedom and justice protected by a constitution. Yohanan Badar of Herut described[46] the differences in the views of the spokesmen of the Religious Bloc—one favored a constitution at a later date (Yizhaq Meir Lewin); a second opposed it forever (David Meir Loewenstein); a third had one view one day and another view on the morrow (Zorah Wahrhaftig). "Where," Badar queried, "is the influence of Torah?" Abraham Haim Shaag of the Religious Bloc even indicated[47] that he was not opposed to the commencement of work on the constitution immediately, since it would take at least thirty years to arrive at agreement. Eri Jabotinsky of Herut argued that the Religious Bloc should even welcome a constitution. Without a constitution the Kneset might legislate on religious matters. Furthermore, without a constitution Arabic was not a privileged language. To demonstrate this he deliberately uttered one sentence in French. His personal view, however, was that Hebrew should be the only tongue,[48] and that the state should be uninational.[49] His party later disassociated itself from the views expressed in his speech except for his conclusion that a written constitution was necessary.[50]

Yakov Klibanov of the General Zionists expressed regret[51] that while the Head of the Government found time to examine the Scriptures to discover that it made no provision for privileged laws, he did not study the writings of American political theorists to discover that a written constitution with judicial review safe-

[45] *Ibid.*, 113th meeting, 740-41.
[46] *Ibid.*, 134th meeting, 1264.
[47] *Ibid.*, 116th meeting, 796.
[48] *Ibid.*, 134th meeting, 1313.
[49] *Ibid.*, 1312.
[50] *Ibid.*, 1332.
[51] *Ibid.*, 117th meeting, 825-26.

guards democracy. Furthermore, if the religious parties compromised their consciences to participate in elections based on a "secular elections law" and to hold portfolios in a government with secularist parties, they ought not find it difficult to make their peace with a state that would be conducted along lines not necessarily traditional in character.

THE FINAL RESOLUTION

Yizhar Harari of the Progressive Party was one of the most temperate discussants of the issues.[52] He favored a written constitution, but he assured the Religious Bloc that he did not necessarily mean to precipitate a Kulturkampf. With a measure of good will and mutual understanding, agreement could be reached. The resolution he proposed was finally approved on June 13, 1950. It read as follows:

> The First Kneset commissions the Committee on Constitution, Law, and Justice, to prepare a proposed constitution for the state. The constitution shall be constructed in chapters in such a way that each one of them shall be a fundamental law by itself. The chapters shall be brought before the Kneset as the committee finishes its work on each, and all the chapters together shall then be combined into a constitution for the state.[53]

By its terms, this resolution affirmed that Israel should have a written constitution. Perhaps this affirmation had some significance. Though it can be repealed by a subsequent Kneset, or simply ignored, it did constitute a mandate to the designated committee to perform the specified task. However, Moshe Sneh, a Mapam leader, immediately proclaimed that the resolution was virtually a denial of a constitution.[54] He said that the fact that the Religious Bloc had abstained from voting for the resolution proved that as a member of the coalition Government it had al-

[52] *Ibid.*, 115th meeting, 776-80.
[53] *Ibid.*, V, 2d Sess., 151st meeting, 1743.
[54] *Ibid.*, 1722.

ready consented to let some chapters be approved while Mapai had assured it that a full constitution would never come into being.

His accusation may have been untrue, but one can hardly avoid the conclusion that the issue of a written constitution was in fact resolved negatively. Since no time limit was placed on the committee to bring forth even one chapter, the matter could be tabled indefinitely.[55] And even if one or more chapters were to be approved by a second or third Kneset, the crucial chapter would be one that would describe how a constitutional provision might enjoy a higher status than an ordinary law. Otherwise, calling it by another name is legally inconsequential. The debate yielded not even a proposal on this problem. Harari himself had to explain that his resolution did not flout his party's platform that a written constitution be drafted.[56] His answer was that his party had not decided the manner in which one should be drafted and his resolution added that.[57] The Mapam press was even more critical.[58]

It may be, however, that the Second Kneset will proceed to carry out the resolution, for in it the ha-Po'el ha-Mizrahi may not be bound by commitments to a Religious Bloc. And ha-Po'el ha-Mizrahi is the only religious party that has recently at least begun to analyze the religious and legal literature of Judaism for guidance on constitutional problems.

Its own organized rabbinate—known as Hever ha-Rabanim—undertook the publication of a series of studies devoted to this subject as well as other religious problems which the establishment of the state precipitated for the observant Jew. Three small volumes were published during the period of the First Kneset and were called *ha-Torah we-ha-Medinah* (The Torah and the

[55] See *Luah ha-Arez* (ha-Arez Calendar) (Tel Aviv, 5711: 1950), p. 76.
[56] See *ha-'Oved ha-Ziyoni,* No. 17, June 28, 1950, p. 2.
[57] *Ibid.*
[58] See editorial, *'Al ha-Mishmar,* June 15, 1950, p. 1.

State).[59] While most of the studies are concerned with civil law, criminal law, and the law of religious observance, a few deal with public law. The latter indicate that ha-Poel ha-Mizrahi will have no difficulty in accepting a democratic constitution—nay, they will deem it a necessary consequence of Torah ideals. The right of the people to legislate by majority vote or through elected representative is vouchsafed.[60] Even the provision that voters shall be eighteen years of age, and lawmakers at least twenty, has roots in the tradition.[61]

With such openmindedness it would seem that, at least with respect to political institutions, ha-Po'el ha-Mizrahi could join in a major effort to draft a constitution.

[59] S. Israeli, ed., 3 vols. (Tel Aviv, 1949, 1950 and 1951.)
[60] Israeli, *ha-Torah we-ha-Medinah,* II, 41-54, 76-88.
[61] *Ibid.,* 55-58.

CHAPTER IX

The Religious Problem

ISRAEL'S LEGAL SYSTEM

From a constitutional point of view, the problem of religion in the state is Israel's most perplexing.[1] If a solution seemed imminent or possible, Israel would probably now have a written constitution. The problem, however, is so baffling because it involves the social and legal order of the land.

Basically the question is: Can a secular state be established with a legal order that is significantly, though only partially, religious in character? And that is the character of Israel's legal order. In fact, the religious character of Israel's legal order is multidenominational. Virtually nothing has been done to change it since independence.[2]

The Provisional Government did name Jewish judges to replace the British ones who left. Arabs too were appointed judges of the District Courts. Several special courts were abolished. But essentially the civil court system is pretty much the same one that

[1] The Jewish Agency's Department for Education and Culture published a volume of essays on the subject entitled *Dat Yisrael u-Medinat Yisrael* (The Religion of Israel and the State of Israel) (New York, 1951).

[2] Even Paragraph 46 of the British Order-in-Council for Palestine (see *Legislation of Palestine—1918-1925*, compiled by N. Bentwich, 2 vols. [Jerusalem, 1926], I, 1-22), which calls for reference to English Common Law and English doctrines of equity in a case of first instance, has not been changed. The religious parties would like a change providing for reference to Jewish law as suggested in Dr. Kohn's draft constitution (*W. H. Proceedings*, Pamphlet II, p. 15).

existed under the mandate, and modifications of both procedural and substantive law have been negligible. The proverbial resistance of lawyers to change has not been tested. They have been required to learn practically nothing new. Yet, while they never welcome radical breaks with the past, they are less responsible for the retention of the status quo than the ideological deadlock between the religious parties and the secularists.

Until the nineteenth century, the canon law of Judaism was generally regarded by most Jews all over the world as binding upon them. During the Middle Ages Jewish communities enjoyed a considerable amount of autonomy in legal affairs. They maintained their own courts and applied their own canon law.[3] Even in antiquity this autonomy was permitted under Babylonian and Persian rule.[4] Particularly with regard to matters of personal status and domestic relations did this law enjoy an almost continuous application and development for several millennia. And in the Turkish Empire it became a well established practice to grant both Christian and Jewish minorities a measure of autonomy at least with regard to personal status law.[5]

The mandatory power made no significant changes in this pattern for Palestine, and to understand Israel's religious problem one can therefore begin with the legal system prevailing at the time of independence.

A British Order-in-Council for Palestine (1922)[6] describes it. Magistrates' courts exercise limited jurisdiction in civil and criminal cases.[7] District courts entertain appeals from magistrates'

[3] S. W. Baron, *Social and Religious History of the Jews*, 2 vols. (New York, 1937), II, 91-97.

[4] Elias J. Bickerman, "Historical Foundations of Post-Biblical Judaism," in *The Jews: Their History, Culture and Religion*, L. Finkelstein, ed., 4 vols. (Philadelphia, 1949), I, 71-73.

[5] F. M. Goadby, *International and Inter-Religious Private Law in Palestine* (Jerusalem, 1926), pp. 100-107.

[6] See Bentwich, *Legislation of Palestine*, 1-22. This order is also reprinted in H. H. Davis, *Constitutions, Electoral Laws, Treaties of States in the Near and Middle East* (Durham, N. C., 1947), pp. 217-39.

[7] Suits and fines involving not more than 100 pounds and penalties of

courts and have original jurisdiction in civil and criminal cases in which judgments or penalties, respectively, are sought in excess of the limits applicable to the lower courts.[8] A court of criminal assize has jurisdiction over capital offenses[9] and a supreme court is the highest appellate court,[10] with original jurisdiction in some cases, e.g. habeas corpus and mandamus.

In addition to these courts there are the courts of the religious communities: Muslim courts, Rabbinic courts, and the ecclesiastical courts of the Christian communities. The scope of their jurisdiction is not uniform. The Muslim courts enjoy exclusive jurisdiction over most Muslims in all matters of personal status[11] and ecclesiastical property. The others enjoy exclusive jurisdiction over only a few matters pertaining to personal status—marriage, divorce, alimony, and the confirmation of wills. Furthermore, they have jurisdiction over only those parties who are enrolled members of the particular religious community.[12] In all other matters pertaining to personal status these courts enjoy concurrent jurisdiction with the district courts, provided that all the parties consent thereto. This is a serious limitation because minors are incapable of legal consent and they are usually necessary parties in cases involving personal status.[13]

---

imprisonment not in excess of one year (sec. 39); see also *Laws of Palestine,* ed. R. H. Drayton, 2 vols. (London, 1934), Vol. II, 898.

[8] Sec. 40. Functions of several special courts were included in the jurisdiction of the District Courts by the Pequdat Batei ha-Mishpat of the State Council of the Provisional Government (*'Iton Rishmi,* No. 7, June 30, 1948, Supp. 1, pp. 17-18).

[9] Sec. 41.

[10] Sec. 43.

[11] Matters of personal status are defined by sec. 51 of the British Order-in-Council as including marriage; divorce; alimony; maintenance; guardianship; legitimation; adoption of minors; inhibitions from dealing with persons who are legally incompetent; successions; wills; legacies and the administration of the property of absent persons.

[12] Sec. 65. This also makes it impossible for a Jewish or Christian foreigner to institute an action for a divorce in Israel. See also M. Zilburg, "Bayat ha-Mazav ha-Ishi ba-Mishpat ha-Arzi Yisraeli" (The Issue of Personal Status in the Law of the Land of Israel), *Qovez Harzaot u-Wikuhim* (Jerusalem, 1938), p. 21.

[13] Kawas *v.* Kawas, Privy Council Appeal No. 41 (1942), 10 Palestine

However, the district courts, in cases involving personal status, are required to apply to Jews and to Christians the law of personal status which prevails in their respective religious communities. The district court does not apply canon adjective law or canon rules of evidence. Thus witnesses incompetent to testify in a Rabbinic court are competent to testify in the district court. But the substantive law of their particular religious community is applied to the parties. As a result, because Jewish canon law does not hold a child born out of wedlock illegitimate, a district court will dismiss a legitimacy proceeding instituted by a Jewish woman against the alleged father of her child. Furthermore, since Jewish canon law makes no provision for the adoption of minors,[14] the district courts are precluded from entertaining adoption proceedings for Jews.

There are exceptions to the general rule that the personal status law of one's religious community is applicable even in the district court. The law of intestate succession, for example, calls for the enforcement of certain Ottoman land laws in all the courts.[15]

Furthermore, the law pertaining to matters that do not involve personal status or ecclesiastical property is a mixture of Ottoman, French, and British Law.[16] The law of corporations, for example, is French and British in origin and character,[17] but rules of property involve Ottoman law as well. However, even in such cases—except where the registry of titles to land may leave no choice—parties may consent in writing to submit their disputes to ecclesiastical courts for resolution in accordance with canon law. This is, in effect, a submission to arbitration.

Law Reports 328 (1943). Perhaps by the appointment of a guardian-ad-litem and with his consent, the problem may be solved.

[14] E. Scheftelowitz, *Jewish Law of Family and Inheritance* (Tel Aviv, 1947), p. 131.

[15] *Laws of Palestine*, II, 1384. See also A. Hoffman, "Rabbinical Courts in Israel," *Jewish Horizon*, June, 1950, p. 6.

[16] K. Hilv, "Die Grundlagen der Rechtsentwicklung in Palestina," *Palestina*, XVth year, No. 1-2 (January-February, 1932), pp. 160-66.

[17] Goadby, *Private Law in Palestine*, p. 209.

Constitutional Problems.—The constitutional problems which this system of law created for the draftsmen of a proposed constitution were numerous. The United Nations General Assembly resolution[18] required that the constitution of Israel respect the law of family and personal status, as well as the law pertaining to ecclesiastical property, of the several religious minorities in the new state. Dr. Kohn, in Article 70 (5) of his draft[19] proposed that "The ecclesiastical courts of the Jewish, Muslim and Christian communities," should have "jurisdiction over matters of personal status and matters of ecclesiastical property." The effect of this provision would be to vest all the ecclesiastical courts with the same jurisdiction that only the Muslim courts now enjoy. Instead of having exclusive jurisdiction over only marriage, divorce, alimony, and the confirmation of wills, the Rabbinic and the Christian courts would have their jurisdiction broadened to include the additional subjects over which the Muslim courts enjoy exclusive jurisdiction, e.g., guardianship, adoption, inheritance. The religious parties have argued that it is anomalous that in an independent Israel the Muslim courts should continue to enjoy a broader jurisdiction than do the Rabbinic courts.[20] However, even religious attorneys are not too anxious to see such a change, for the rules of practice and evidence in the district courts are far more liberal than the rules of the Rabbinic courts. The Rabbinic courts have proposed a revision of their procedure,[21] but the competency of women and non-Jews as witnesses is far from established, and in many cases they are the only witnesses available.

[18] "The family law and personal status of the various minorities and their religious interests, including endowments, shall be respected" (Part I, C, Chap. 2; see *supra,* p. 10-11).

[19] *W. H. Proceedings,* Pamphlet II, p. 14.

[20] A. Hoffman, "Rabbinical Courts," *Jewish Horizon,* June, 1950, p. 7.

[21] See the "Taqanot ha-Diyun be-Vatei ha-Din be-Erez Yisrael" (Procedural Amendments in the Courts of the Land of Israel) of the Chief Rabbinate (1943), discussed in A. H. Friemann, "ha-Taqanot ha-Hadashot Shel ha-Rabanut ha-Rashit" (The New Rules of the Chief Rabbinate), *Sinai,* 7th year, Nos. 10-11 (1944), pp. 254-63.

Therefore, even religious attorneys, to satisfy their own professional interests, often prefer the use of the district courts which at least apply Jewish substantive law in matters of personal status while ignoring the Jewish law of evidence. They also frown upon the failure of judges in the Rabbinic courts to write opinions, which failure makes it difficult to ascertain the rules of law.[22] Appeals to the Chief Rabbinate from decisions of the Rabbinic courts are also thus made more difficult to resolve. However, secularists contend that even the substantive law requires far greater modernization than the Rabbinic courts are prepared to make in the foreseeable future. They therefore seek a civil law applicable to personal status which the district courts will apply, while the Rabbinic courts enjoy only concurrent jurisdiction even in the matters of marriage, divorce, alimony and the confirmation of wills, when the parties consent thereto.

Quite independent of the problem of liberalizing Rabbinic law and modernizing its procedure, there is also the problem of a uniform law for all Jews. While the British Order-in-Council recognized but one Rabbinic law, there were in fact two rules with regard to polygamy. Ashkenazi Jews frowned upon the practice while Sephardi Jews did not. The case of Attorney General v. Melnik[23] dealt with the problem. The defendant was charged with bigamy—a felony. His defense was that the law governing his personal status permitted him to have more than one wife. The Court sought the opinion of Chief Rabbi Isaac Herzog who advised that the bigamous marriage was not void by Rabbinic law. The prohibition against polygamy was established by a ban of Rabbi Gershom almost a millennium ago, but the ban was applicable only to Ashkenazi Jews who accepted that Rabbi's authority. Sephardi Jews had never accepted it and though the de-

[22] See S. B. Feldman, "'Al Shilton ha-Mishpat ha-'Ivri ba-Medinah" (On the Sovereignty of Hebrew Law in the State), *ha-Hed,* 24th year, No. 9 (Sivan, 5709: June, 1949), p. 18. The highest Rabbinic court, however, has since instituted publication of its opinions in *Ozar Pisqei Din* (1950).

[23] Criminal Appeal No. 85 (1938), 6 Palestine Law Reports 34 (1939).

fendant was an Ashkenazi and might be subject to the ban, his second marriage was valid.

With the recent immigration of principally Oriental Jews, who had not accepted the ban, the Kneset could not long defer the question of polygamous marriages. And it did take action,[24] as it did with regard to child marriages which are also common among Orientals.[25]

The religious parties want traditional Jewish law to become the law of the state in all matters: civil, criminal, and public. Their argument has a strong nationalist appeal. Why should a Jewish state rely on Ottoman or Napoleonic or British law when Jews have a great jurisprudence of their own! Here too, many scholars are busily engaged in research projects to point out the precedents in Jewish law for all existing statutes and rules.[26] The Harvard Law School–Israel Cooperative Research for Israel's Legal Development also had under consideration a succession bill for Israel based to a large extent on Jewish law which, quoting from the introduction, "embodies our great tradition which must be revived and continued as one of the treasures of our national culture."[27] Some religious jurists concede that Jewish law could hardly become the basis for a modern penal code. But in most other respects, they contend, Jewish law is adequate for a modern society. Furthermore, they do not want Israel to be a secularist state. Secularists, however, oppose the use of a legal system based on religious authority. They also point to the difficulties involved in the amendment of Jewish law. Changes by judicial interpretation are slow, and changes by the convocation of a supreme Rabbinic body, like a Sanhedrin, may have to await the advent of a Messiah.

[24] *Sefer ha-Huqim, 5711*, p. 248. [25] *Sefer ha-Huqim, 5710*, pp. 286-87.

[26] The Ministry of Justice itself has a division for this purpose. For a full discussion of the problem see Z. Wahrhaftig, "Legal Problems in the State of Israel," *Igeret la-Golah*, No. 18-19 (November-December, 1949), pp. 2-10.

[27] Unpublished text available at the Law School of Harvard University, Cambridge, Massachusetts.

Constitutional Proposals.—Dr. Kohn's draft proposed in Article 77, that "future legislation in Israel should be guided by the basic principles of Jewish law." Dr. Kohn, in a personal interview, revealed that he had in mind a result comparable to that achieved by Gierke for German law. This, however, would hardly satisfy all the religious parties, for *principles* of law are not *rules* of law. Furthermore, the civil courts would retain exclusive jurisdiction over civil and criminal cases. However, the secularists objected with equal fervor to reliance in cases of first instance upon anything other than the broadest humanitarian ideals articulated in Jewish literature.

Professor Vitta proposed a compromise to the Committee on the Constitution of the State Council of the Provisional Government. However, his proposals were hardly a compromise between the extreme demands of both sides. They were rather a compromise between the retention of the status quo and the demands of the secularists.

By way of introduction,[28] he suggested that the religious courts should not be called ecclesiastic courts but courts of the religious communities. This would be the first time, he indicated, that the Muslims would be designated a religious community. Theretofore only the communities of Jews and Christians were thus called. Second, all of the existing nine Christian communities should be enumerated in the written constitution. Theretofore they were enumerated only in the inheritance law. Vitta, however, did not consider what would happen with new religious communities[29] which Jews, Muslims, or Christians might seek to organize and for whose recognition they would ultimately petition. Thus, for example, liberal Jews in America, through their organized Rab-

[28] *W. H. Proceedings,* Pamphlet V, p. 29.

[29] The organization of added Jewish religious communities was discussed in several cases. Rokach *v.* District Commissioner of Lydda, High Court No. 5, Palestine Law Reports 191 (1942); Central Agudath-Israel of Palestine *v.* Chief Secretary, Government of Palestine, High Court No. 110, 9 Palestine Law Reports 572 (1942); and Vaad Adat Ashkenazim *v.* Beit Din Hassidim, 9 Palestine Law Reports 715 (1942).

binate, the Central Conference of American Rabbis, have already protested that they would have no right to solemnize marriages in Israel and, unless new Jewish religious communities can be formed, they and their colleagues will never have this right. Nor did Vitta consider what would happen with religious communities that do not provide for divorce and regard it as an exclusive function of the state, e.g., Protestants.[30]

Vitta agreed with Kohn that the judges of the religious courts should be appointed and removed by the president in consultation with the Minister of Religions. But Kohn had proposed that the supreme bodies of the religious communities make the nominations. In the case of the removal of a judge, in addition to the approval of these supreme bodies, there should be required the concurrence of two-thirds of all the legislators. Vitta, on the other hand, proposed that for each group of courts there should be established a special committee.[31] Each committee should consist of the Minister of Justice, the senior Judge of the Supreme Court, and three judges of the particular religious community involved, who should be selected in a manner most suitable for that group. For the Jewish community, for example, the Chief Rabbinate might make the appointments. These committees would promulgate the rules and regulations pertaining to the courts of their denomination. These rules would apply to the appointment of new judges, their removal, transfer, discipline, salaries, and pensions. Vitta recommended the inclusion of the Minister of Justice and the senior Judge of the Supreme Court because in this manner a measure of coordination with the civil court system would be realized not only in the appointment of judges but also in matters of judicial discipline. The autonomy of the religious community would not be affected, for it would still have three votes out of five. Furthermore, the integration of these courts into the general

[30] See Paul Blanshard, "Israel: Church and State," *The Nation*, CLXX, No. 21 (May 27, 1950), 522.

[31] *W. H. Proceedings*, Pamphlet V, p. 30.

court system with regard to their fiscal requirements would be expedited.

To avoid any further provocation of Israel's neighboring Arab states by flouting the provision of the United Nations resolution with respect thereto,[32] he deemed it advisable to leave the Muslim courts in status quo.[33] But what of the Jewish and Christian ecclesiastical courts? Dr. Kohn's original proposal was to give these courts the same powers that the Muslim courts enjoy. Dr. Kohn subsequently proposed that the status quo under the mandate be retained. Thereafter he thought it best to leave the entire matter out of the constitution. Professor Vitta indicated that this last solution should be resorted to only if the debate on the subject in the Constituent Assembly should be so sharp as to disrupt its work. Otherwise, the basic principles should be agreed upon and set forth in the constitution.

If, however, ecclesiastical courts were given exclusive jurisdiction over all matters of personal status, their jurisdiction would be increased, not limited. Second, if no distinction were drawn between citizens and aliens, or at least residents and nonresidents, and one's denomination were to be the sole basis for jurisdiction so that Jewish and Christian ecclesiastical courts would have exclusive jurisdiction over all Jews and Christians, respectively, who were physically present in Israel, then these courts would have even broader powers than the Muslim courts, which have jurisdiction only over Muslims who are citizens or nationals of a country whose law of personal status calls for the application of Muslim law. For these reasons Vitta regarded Dr. Kohn's draft as totally unsatisfactory.[34] But he conceded that a proposal acceptable to all Jews is not easy to find.

The late Dr. Abraham Hayyim Freiman, of the Hebrew University, supported the proposal that the Jewish courts have exclu-

[32] *Supra*, p. 124.

[33] *W. H. Proceedings*, Pamphlet V, p. 31.

[34] *Ibid.*, p. 32.

sive jurisdiction over matters of personal status but urged that these courts should also consist of judges of the civil courts.[35] This would help to eliminate the hostility of the civil courts to the religious courts and would contribute to a gradual blending of secularist and religious viewpoints by the jurists. Others had proposed concurrent jurisdiction on all matters of personal status for both the civil and religious courts.[36] Still others had proposed exclusive jurisdiction for the religious courts over marriage and divorce, leaving other matters of personal status to come under the exclusive jurisdiction of the civil courts.[37]

Professor Vitta himself proposed that first there ought to be established the principle that residence, not citizenship, determine whether a religious court has jurisdiction.[38] Furthermore, while the existing jurisdiction of the Muslim courts should not be altered and all their judges should be clerics, the jurisdiction of the Jewish and Christian courts should be limited to marriage and divorce.[39] Judges of the civil courts should also act as members of the religious courts. In all other matters of personal status, civil courts should have jurisdiction. However, when they so act, they should apply the law which the ecclesiastical court would find applicable thereto, unless the parties were nonresidents. For nonresidents the law of their domicile would be applicable. Full details, however, about the law applicable to nonresidents, or the law applicable in a case where the parties were of two different religious communities or of none, should be set forth in a statute. A statute should also set forth under what circumstances the senior Judge of the Supreme Court shall decide whether the civil or the religious courts have jurisdiction. Dr. Kohn had thus provided, but he also provided that the judge should seek the opinion of the religious courts. Vitta felt that such a rule or similar rules should be set forth in a statute, not the constitution.[40]

[35] *Ibid.*
[36] *Ibid.*
[37] *Ibid.*
[38] *Ibid.*, pp. 32-33.
[39] *Ibid.*, p. 33.
[40] *Ibid.*

THE OUTLOOK FOR CHANGE

Several objections to the jurisdiction of the Rabbinic courts have already been suggested. These range from a general ideological objection to any kind of religiously sanctioned law to the comparatively minor objection that the procedure in the religious courts is archaic. The principal difficulty, however, is that women do not enjoy full equality under Rabbinic law.[41] In almost no system of law do men and women enjoy full equality in family law. But Jewish religious law adds certain disabilities which no longer contribute to the protection of the so-called weaker sex. For example, a widow, whose husband was childless, cannot remarry without having received a formal release from a surviving brother-in-law. The same restriction does not apply to a widower. Furthermore, the Rabbinic courts can exercise coercion against males who are before the court and cause them to divorce their wives for cause, but they cannot terminate the marriage of a woman at her behest and for cause if her husband is in another country. They could do so, however, on the application of a husband against an absentee wife.

Dr. Freiman has written a book on the history of marriage according to Jewish law since the redaction of the Talmud, and in the appendix[42] he collates many proposals which would have virtually eliminated the features objectionable to Jewish women, without flouting the tradition. None of these proposals has ever been universally accepted, because in one generation or another some prominent rabbi has uttered a violent protest and even threatened a ban.

[41] The extent to which even religious leaders feel that the traditional law must be revised to permit equality of females with males, and non-Jews with Jews, can be gleaned from S. Federbush, "Malchut u-Srarah be-Yisrael" (Sovereignty and Power in Israel), *ha-Doar,* 13 Nisan, 5710: April 30, 1950, pp. 537-40, and M. Bar-Ilan, "Tazkir" (Memorandum), *Yavneh,* III (Nisan, 5709: April, 1949), 32. Dr. Federbush suggests that the traditional inequality applies only to matters of religious observance.

[42] *Seder Qidushin we-Nisuin* (The Order of Betrothal and Marriage) (Jerusalem, 1945), pp. 385-97.

It is for this reason that progressive women in Israel have good and sufficient grounds for assuming that unless the exclusiveness of the jurisdiction of the rabbis over marriage and divorce is ended the law will not be liberalized.[43] That is why they are opposed to Dr. Kohn's proposal in his draft constitution. A summary of virtually all the criticisms are set forth in Haim Greenberg's "Notes on the Israeli Constitution."[44] Greenberg argues that according to Kohn's draft the state is obligated to consider every citizen as belonging to one of three (or more) religious communities. If he refuses to apply to the recognized religious courts, he has no way of legalizing or registering his marriage or the birth of a child; he has no one to grant him a divorce; and it is not clear who will be responsible for probating his will and dividing his inheritance among his heirs if he dies intestate.

Why should the state force a citizen to accept a personal status which he himself does not care to have? Why should there not be a general civil jurisdiction for anyone seeking to marry or be divorced on conditions a particular church fails to recognize?

Furthermore, what will be the status in Israel of non-Orthodox synagogues and rabbis? Will marriages and divorces authorized by such rabbis be considered valid by the Jewish courts, which will probably consist of Orthodox judges?

Greenberg recommends that the state set up civil courts and civil procedures dealing with personal status for all its citizens:

> This would not preclude the functioning of religious courts for those citizens who might wish to live under their jurisdiction. Such courts would be partly private, partly public, institutions, maintained by

[43] Possibly it was in the hope of seeing such a liberalization take place that Dr. Freiman suggested that judges of the civil courts also sit in the religious courts with rabbis. Impatience with the Rabbinate of Israel for its failure to contribute to a solution of many legal problems is expressed by even religious leaders. See S. Z. Shragai, "Fundamentals of a Torah State," *Jewish Horizon*, XII, No. 9 (May, 1950), 8, and in *Igeret la-Golah*, No. 24 (May, 1950), pp. 36-39.

[44] *The Jewish Frontier*, XVI, No. 5 (May, 1949), 36-38.

those citizens who want them and are willing to support them. A marriage recognized by such a court would also be recognized by the State; a divorce granted by such a court would be valid in the eyes of the State; and if heirs agree to allow a religious court to divide their inheritance among them (after taxes) there is no reason for the State to interfere—just as no State would prevent its citizens from settling certain disputes by voluntary arbitration rather than in the civil courts.

Mr. Greenberg ignored what Vitta and Kohn had already pointed out, that for political reasons Jews will not be able to curtail the jurisdiction of Muslim courts for many years to come. With regard to Christians and Jews, it is more realistic to hope for civil marriage and divorce. But the real issue is not only what court shall have jurisdiction but what law shall be applied in the court exercising jurisdiction. Shall the civil courts apply a new set of rules of law to the parties before them—a set of rules determined by the Kneset? If they apply the rules of the religious courts which might have had jurisdiction over the parties, Greenberg's objections will not have been answered. If they apply a new and special set of rules, then there has been added to the already numerous jurisdictions a civil one which compounds the chaos in every religious community. It would be as if someone recommended as a panacea for the divorce problem in the United States a federal system of divorce, in addition to those of the forty-eight states rather than in lieu of the forty-eight separate jurisdictions.

Existing mores do affect the law. If the Kneset does establish a new family law to replace the old, will it follow Jewish, Christian or Muslim mores, or ignore all three? And would such a law so offend in the religious communities that those who abide by it will be ineligible for intermarriage with communicants of existing religious bodies? How will this affect the development of homogeneity in an already dangerously heterogeneous community?[45]

[45] A reply to Mr. Greenberg by the writer is contained in "The American *v.* Israeli Rabbinate," *Jewish Horizon,* XIII, No. 6 (1951), 5-7.

One issue with regard to family law which the First Kneset resolved was to make the practice of child marriage a crime. The debate was truly an impassioned one.[46] But a law was finally approved prohibiting the marriage of girls under 17 years of age.[47] The controversy is not too relevant to either the State's structure or the party cleavages, for among European Jews in recent decades the early marriage of girls was very uncommon. The Religious Bloc, therefore, gave only token support to the Oriental Jews who resisted the change. They served rather as mediators between the spokesmen of the majority sentiment and the intransigent minority. This was also true when the Kneset, in 1951, abolished one defense to a criminal complaint on polygamy, to wit: that the law of one's personal status permitted it.[48] It is when more radical changes—such as the introduction of civil marriage and divorce, the direct abolition of the levirate law, or the adoption of procedures that will in effect abolish it—may be sought that the battle may begin in earnest.

STATE SUPPORT FOR RELIGIOUS COMMUNITIES

Related to the problem of the ecclesiastic courts is the problem of the State's financial support of the religious communities. If the courts of these communities are an integral part of the legal system of the country, then, of course, the State must bear the burden of maintaining them. This it does. In effect, however, it

[46] *Divrei ha-Kneset,* IV, 2d Sess., 109th meeting, 638-40; *ibid.,* 110th meeting, 649-69; *ibid.,* 115th meeting, 1819-20; and *ibid.,* 173rd meeting, 2414-17. Valid the marriages will be, but the persons responsible will be punished for crime. A good English summary of the debate on child marriages is found in *Igeret la-Golah,* No. 22 (March, 1950), pp. 10-14. It appears that the Chief Rabbinate also wanted child marriages prohibited by the criminal law because of the difficulties involved in making the amendment by a change of canon law. See an article by Chief Rabbi Herzog's secretary, J. Goldman, "Child Marriages," *Jewish Horizon,* XII, No. 10 (June, 1950), 12. Will this serve as a pattern for the manner of making further amendments of Jewish canon law? It did in the abolition of polygamy.

[47] *Sefer ha-Huqim, 5711,* p. 248.

[48] *Ibid.*

constitutes a subsidy to religion. The clerics, who are judges in these courts, receive their salaries out of public funds and find it possible to serve as religious functionaries in other capacities as well. But what about state support of religious work other than judicial services?

In the debates of the Committee on the Constitution of the State Council of the Provisional Government the committee's chairman, Dr. Wahrhaftig, pointed out[49] that there are countries like Mexico and the USSR which separate church and state because of a hostile attitude toward religion. Other countries, however, separate the two because of a favorable attitude toward religion and their desire to avoid interference by the state in matters of faith. This is true of the English-speaking countries. But these countries were not socialistic. Taxes therein were always comparatively low and religious institutions were maintained by voluntary gifts. On the other hand, in countries where the economy is subject to greater governmental control, where taxes are very high, and where most community needs are met by the state, religious institutions cannot derive adequate support from voluntary gifts. Certainly in a socialist state, almost all social needs are fulfilled out of taxes. Wherefore, then, should the State of Israel overlook the religious needs of its constituents?

Dr. Kohn's draft contained no provision whatever for the support of religious communities by the state. Nor did it prohibit such support.[50] But at the first session of the Kneset a bill was passed which dealt directly with the problem. By this bill, the State undertook to subsidize the local Jewish religious coun-

[49] *W. H. Proceedings*. Pamphlet I, p. 19.

[50] "Since the drafters (Dr. Kohn and his colleagues) were familiar with most, if not all, of the above (American, Irish, Mexican, and Weimar) constitutions, one may suspect that although a state supported Church may never be established, the drafters left possible such a development, and hoped thereby, to avoid controversy with those desirous of having an official religion designated." E. M. Million and A. S. Katz, "Provisions on Religious Freedom in the Draft Israeli Constitution," *N.Y.U. Law Quar. Rev.*, No. 24 (1949), p. 860.

cils to the extent of one-third of their budgets, leaving the other two-thirds to be raised by the local authorities.[51]

This statute established a principle of tremendous constitutional significance. The state acknowledged its responsibility to meet the religious needs of the community. The religious parties frankly contend that this is only one step in the right direction. They anticipate even more generous support of organized religion in Israel. To most Americans even the one step is shocking. But to Jews in Israel—most of whom come from European countries where state support of organized religion is the rule rather than the exception—the statute was hardly regarded as a dangerous one. As a matter of fact, it received the support of Mapai.

The Muslim and Christian religious communities are also receiving some assistance. The budget of the Ministry of Religions provides for it.[52] In the summer of 1951, there were 193 Muslim religious officials in Israel who were paid by the government or out of the proceeds of the Waqf administration.[53] These included not only qadhis (religious judges) but also imams (prayer leaders) and preachers.

RELIGIOUS AND SECULAR SCHOOLS

State support of Israel's schools is another problem which involves the role of religion in the state. For many years before independence there existed in Israel many school systems for Jews. The largest was that known as the Zerem ha-Klali, the "general" schools, which were hardly secularist in character since religious instruction was given daily. Its instructors may not have been as pious as the instructors in the two orthodox sys-

[51] *Divrei ha-Kneset,* II, 1st Sess., 67th meeting, 1303-7, and *Sefer ha-Huqim, 5709,* pp. 150-51.

[52] *Ibid.,* p. 222. For a discussion of the principle of equality in this connection, see *supra,* pp. 83-84.

[53] *The Arabs in Israel,* Pamphlet of the Israel Office of Information (January, 1952), p. 23.

tems, but they could hardly satisfy a Marxist. Then there were the Mizrahi system, orthodox in character, and the Agudat Yisrael system—still more orthodox. In the latter, Bible and Talmud were virtually the only subjects of instruction and Yiddish was as prominent a language as Hebrew. There were also a number of Talmudei Torah and Yeshivot which were even more extremely fundamentalist than the Mizrahi and Agudat Yisrael schools. The mildly socialistic schools were under the control of the Merkaz ha-Hinuh Shel Zerem 'Ovdim, a unit of the Histadrut, while a few extremely socialistic schools were run by the Mapam in several of its collective settlements. There were also private schools, one of which, the French Alliance system, was maintained by a group of Jews outside of Israel.

At the beginning of the school year 1950-51, about a third of the children were enrolled in the "general" schools, another third in the Histadrut schools, a fourth in the Mizrahi and Agudat schools, and the remainder in the schools of extremists and in the private schools which received no government subsidies but met the requirements of the compulsory education law.[54]

The partisan character of the school system was the subject of considerable criticism in World Zionist congresses, and the perpetuation of the condition in the State of Israel has troubled many.[55] As a matter of fact, the Histadrut undertook an intensive campaign to enroll in its schools more of its members' children, thus to prepare them for unflinching loyalty to its ideology. It even introduced some religious instruction to satisfy those of its members who were orthodox. This trend might have been strengthened by the growth of one faction within the Histadrut—ha-'Oved ha-Dati (Religious Worker)—and by the Histadrut's avowed purpose to gain members from among the new immigrants, most of whom are orthodox.

[54] For the exact figures for 1950, see *Government Yearbook, 5711*, pp. 438-42.

[55] Mark M. Krug, "Education for Disunity," *Congress Weekly*, XVI, No. 29 (November 14, 1949), 8.

The Compulsory Education Law,[56] which was introduced into the Kneset by Israel's Minister of Education, Zalman Shazar (Mapai), did not alter the situation. Large expenditures for new schools, classrooms, and additional teachers were authorized. But parents retained the power to choose the type of school to which they wanted to send their children. Four "trends" were recognized for state support—the "General," Histadrut, Mizrahi and Agudat Yisrael.[57] Thus, in effect, the state undertook to support party school systems.

The General Zionists and Progressives opposed the law.[58] They expressed their disapproval of a law which would make it increasingly difficult to attain national unity. The educational system, they contended, should be above politics. Shazar retorted that since Mapai was in control of the Government, a unified system would normally reflect a Mapai orientation and, therefore, his party was even being generous in not taking advantage of its opportunity.[59]

An American would find it difficult to accept the principle of party school systems. Most Americans, for example, unequivocally oppose state support of denominational schools. They resist interference by organized religion in either the subjects of instruction or the methods of school administration. Even more violently would they oppose partisan politics in education—a Republican school system or a Democratic school system. But the Kneset debate revealed that the curriculum of a Jewish school makes it almost impossible to do anything but have party schools. For the schools must teach Hebrew literature, and even the secularists do not eliminate the Bible from courses in Hebrew literature. The schools must also teach Jewish history. Yet, there can be no agreement as to how these subjects will be taught.

[56] *Sefer ha-Huqim, 5709,* pp. 287-94.

[57] The law mentions these trends but does not define or describe them.

[58] *Divrei ha-Kneset,* II, 1st Sess., 58th meeting, 1100-1102, and 60th meeting, 1152-54.

[59] *Ibid.,* 1160.

How will teachers describe the exodus from Egypt? As historic fact or myth? As a miraculous event or the expulsion of lepers, according to Torah or Freud? And what was the Talmud? Nonsensical dialectic studded with sophistry or the treasure house of Jewish religious, legal, and ethical insights? Is the Bible man-made literature or divinely revealed and inspired? And is Weizmann, Gordon, or Reines[60] the patron saint of Zionism? Even if one could prepare a completely objective course, what kind of teachers would teach it? Must they be without conviction, frigid tutors whose instruction reveals no personal bias?

That is why Israel found it so difficult to have public schools of one pattern for all Jewish children. Without a variety of schools—a variety that satisfied the secularists, the religionists, and the center groups—the State might have interfered with the freedom of parents to educate their children. That is why Palestine Jews developed, long before independence, several school systems with different orientations, all of which were supported by the Kneset Israel.

Such a multiple system of education means that in the Ministry of Education there are men chosen because of their affiliation with the secularists, the religious community, and the center. The same ministry has Muslim and Christian representatives to supervise the education of Muslim and Christian youth, who by the terms of the law have won recognition for their "trends." There is as yet a great dearth of Arab teachers, and one of the first projects that the Ministry had to undertake was the establishment of an Arab Teachers' Seminary. Until there is a greater supply of Arab teachers the full implementation of the compulsory education law with respect to Arabs will not be possible.[61]

Nonetheless, progress in this direction has been made. While

[60] Gordon was the philosopher of Labor Zionism while Reines was the philosopher of Religious Zionism.

[61] M. Assaf, "The Non-Jewish Population of Israel," *Israel*, January, 1950, p. 29.

the number of Arab schools in December, 1948, was only 46 with 186 teachers and 7,147 pupils, there were at the end of the school year 1950-51, 102 government schools with 628 teachers and about 26,000 pupils.[62] These pupils include almost 9,000 girls. Contrary to expectation, the introduction of coeducation aroused little opposition.[63] Another reform was the abolition of corporal punishment. The Arab private schools, which are maintained principally by foreign missions and church institutions, have approximately 4,500 pupils.

It would seem, however, that some integration of the school systems could be effected. Plans for a unitary system are often proposed.[64] Even David Pinkas,[65] Mizrahi leader, favored integration to the extent that there would be only two systems—religious and secularist—and each without party connections. His proposal was adopted by the Second Kneset.

An interesting problem arose, however, when the teachers of the Mizrahi school system joined the Histadrut.[66] In Israel, thus far, most benefits that are in the category of "social security" are dispensed by the unions federated in the Histadrut and not by the state. The religious teachers, therefore, felt impelled to join the Histadrut, though the latter is opposed to the school system which they serve. Whether this affiliation will affect the administration and curriculum of the Mizrahi school system—as was predicted by Mizrahi party leaders—remains to be seen.

[62] *The Arabs in Israel*, p. 20. [63] *Ibid.*, pp. 20-21.

[64] See I. Shapiro, "Yuqam Bet-Sefer Meuhad be-Yisrael" (Let There Be Established a Unified School in Israel), *ha-Arez*, 26 Tishrei, 5710: October 19, 1949, p. 4, and Shapiro, "Bayat ha-Hinuh ha-Meuhad be-Yisrael" (The Issue of Unified Education in Israel), *ha-Doar*, 2 Marheshvan, 5711: October 13, 1950, p. 1087.

[65] *Divrei ha-Kneset*, VIII, 3d Sess., 226th meeting, 1084.

[66] There is a very strong movement within the ha-Po'el ha-Mizrahi to join with the Histadrut generally. One of the leaders of this movement, David Intrilligator, expressed his views in "The Place of Hapoel Hamizrachi in the Working Community," *Hagesher*, III, No. 23-24 (April-June, 1950), 19-22, and No. 25-26 (July-September, 1950), 19-22. See also A. Toshav, "ha-Tesisah ba-Miflagot" (The Ferment in the Parties), *ha-Doar*, 17 Adar I, 5711: February 23, 1951, p. 308.

The incident, however, helps to show that all the roads are not to divisiveness alone.

The problem which precipitated the resignation of the Government in 1951 and the need for new elections pertained to the education of children in the immigrants' reception and work camps. The United Religious Bloc had been complaining for months that in the immigrants' centers coercion was exercised against religious immigrants to make them register their children in Histadrut schools.[67] This was accomplished, they asserted, by vesting jurisdiction over the schools of such centers in the Mapai-dominated Department of Culture, which, it was charged, even prohibited access to the camps by rabbis or religious teachers.

When an investigating commission substantiated the charges,[68] an agreement was reached within the Government[69] as to how to correct the situation. The Religious Bloc, however, was dissatisfied with both the interpretation and the implementation of this agreement by the Head of the Government and his party. It claimed that the Head of the Government was limiting the agreement to the immigrants' reception centers and not applying it to the work centers, the second stage in the absorption of immigrants.[70] At these work centers, it was charged, Mapai was again using coercion to get the children into Histadrut schools, in many of which it was even introducing religious instruction. The crisis was followed by the resignation of the Government,[71] whose ministers continued to function pending new elections. What is most significant, however, is that the problem of religion in the state, in this instance the problem of education, was the principal cause for the fall of the coalition Government.

[67] *Divrei ha-Kneset,* IV, 2d Sess., 120th meeting, 883-85.

[68] Its report was dated 22 Iyar, 5710 (May 9, 1950). The full report was published in *She'arim,* Special Supplement, June 29, 1950. A brief summary may be found in *ha-Arez,* XXXII, No. 9370 (June 12, 1950), 1.

[69] *Divrei ha-Kneset,* IV, 2d Sess., 126th meeting, 1015.

[70] *Ibid.,* VIII, 3d Sess., 225th meeting, 1041.

[71] *Ibid.,* 227th meeting, 1109.

OBSERVANCE OF RELIGIOUS RITUALS BY THE STATE

To what extent will the observance of religious rituals be mandatory in the conduct of all state affairs and the maintenance of all government institutions? And to what extent will such observance be enacted from individuals?

Even the religious parties have disavowed any intention to exact religious observance from individuals. With the exception of a fanatical but negligible minority in Israel, all groups concede that no person will be compelled to observe the dietary laws, refrain from smoking on the Sabbath, or perform, or abstain from performing, such deeds as are required by the ordinances of Judaism.

However, the religious parties do insist on such observance in all government affairs and government institutions, and in a state which controls much of the economy of the land it is inevitable that there be some interference with one's wishes even in matters of ritual observance. If army messes serve only kosher food, a soldier is technically free to eat elsewhere. But practically speaking his choice is not very great. If busses, government owned, do not operate to the beaches on Saturdays, one is technically free to bathe on the Sabbath. But practically speaking, when one lives far away and cannot afford the fare of a privately owned taxicab, one cannot fulfill one's wishes.

That is why there is such great opposition to the demands of the religious parties that all religious observances be imposed on the government, qua government. Yet, it is noteworthy that one of the very first official acts of the Provisional Government was to proclaim the national holidays.[72] These are called "Days of Rest" and include all the Sabbaths and major festivals of Judaism. The minor festivals, on which, according to Orthodox Jewish laws, all forms of activity are permitted, were not included. Furthermore, the New Year holiday is a two-day festival —again in accordance with orthodox Jewish law. The two-day

[72] *'Iton Rishmi,* No. 4, Supp. 1 (June 9, 1948), p. 12.

observance is a tradition based on the manner of computing the intercalation of lunar months in ancient times, and liberal Jews commemorate the tradition with a one-day rather than a two-day observance. Yet the law of the Provisional Government met with the unanimous approval of all the parties represented—even Mapam. Provision, however, was made for permission to non-Jews to observe their own Sabbaths and festivals. It is not yet clear whether this provision means that non-Jews will have an added day of rest or may choose another day in lieu of Saturday.[73] It is noteworthy that the law does not refer to these days as days of "spiritual elevation." Professor Konvitz[74] had criticized the incorporation of such a phrase in Dr. Kohn's draft constitution, and its omission in the statute may be significant.

Beyond the question of the national holidays, however, agreement ends. As already indicated, it was the representative of Agudat Yisrael in the Committee on the Constitution of the State Council of the Provisional Government who made the broadest demands for religious observances by, and in, all state agencies. And since the establishment of the State a number of demands were fulfilled.

The calendar used in all official publications and all statutes is the Hebrew calendar. State anniversaries are also based on the Hebrew calendar. No import permits were issued for nonkosher meat, as the very limited foreign exchange was not made available for this purpose. Post offices did not deliver food packages during the Passover festival, lest they contain items the consumption of which was prohibited on the holiday. These items might become nonusable even after the feast had ended, if title was acquired by the consignees during the feast. This represented consideration for the welfare of observant Jews but disturbed the irreligious. Army messes were provided with only kosher food

[73] See unpublished "Memorandum of Russian Lawyers on Proposed Israeli Constitution," in the library of the American Jewish Congress.

[74] M. Konvitz, "The Bill of Rights in the Draft Constitution for Israel," *The Reconstructionist*, XIV, No. 20 (February 4, 1949), 12-14.

and Sabbath observance was instituted in all military installations. Under the supervision of the chaplains all of this was accomplished, and more. "Mezuzot" were placed on doorposts, dishes were ritualistically cleansed, the food was prepared under rabbinic supervision, services were conducted, and religious supplies made available.

Stern opposition to all this was voiced in the Mapam press.[75] The argument of even the secularists in the Government is one based on the need for national unity. They say that it is not injurious to anyone's interest to make it possible for all government employees to eat in government cafeterias, or all hospital patients to eat the hospital's food, or all school children to eat in school lunchrooms, or all soldiers to eat in army messes. They further say that to respect the folkways or religious convictions of a minority in a democracy is not inconsistent with the doctrine of separation of church and state.

One may argue that it is possible to arrange for two kinds of messes in the army, in hospitals, and in all other government facilities. Yet the segregation that would then come to pass, particularly in the army, would be most undesirable.

The operation of public utilities on the Sabbath is another problem of great concern. Many communities exercise local option with regard to the running of busses. But the State cannot long defer decision on what will be state-owned harbors and, generally, the enjoyment of franchises granted by the Government. Electric power is available seven days a week, and in many cities the restaurants, cafes and other places of business are open on the Sabbath. The picture is a very confusing one and as yet it is difficult to predict how far the State will go in its acceptance of Jewish law as its guide in such matters. As with the problem of the courts, the extremists on both ends will have to cultivate greater mutual respect and tolerance before a constitutional pattern will emerge.

[75] Editorial, *'Al ha-Mishmar,* February 1, 1950, p. 1.

Thus far, on the Sabbath, ships are not permitted to dock and the one existing railroad does not operate. Airplanes, however, do land at the Lydda Airport. Army vehicles, if driven on the Sabbath, must bear special authorization.

Even during the days of the Provisional Government a crisis almost developed over the importation of nonkosher meat from the United States.[76] The savings to the Government would have been large and the Head of the Government favored the purchases. The religious parties, however, argued that the result would be discrimination against their constituents. The supply of kosher meat would always be smaller proportionately than the supply of nonkosher meat, since the cost of importing the former would be greater.

With regard to none of these issues can it be said that any progress was made in the direction of greater understanding among the parties of the left or right.

[76] *M.H.H. Proceedings*, 31st meeting, December 16, 1948, pp. 20-27.

CHAPTER X

Territorial and Military Problems

SPECIFICATION OF BOUNDARIES

Whether or not the Israeli constitution should specify the boundaries of the State emerged as an important problem during the earliest days of the republic. To many Americans, perhaps, the question would not appear to be important. The Constitution of the United States does not describe the territory to which it applies. But that constitution was originally regarded as a compact between sovereign states, whose boundaries constituted a problem to be resolved by agreements between the states or by litigation initiated before the Supreme Court. The federal government was to govern territories belonging to it from which new states would be carved,[1] and while no statement was made of the power to acquire new territories, the Supreme Court inferred this power from several others. Generally, it may be said that the failure to specify boundaries in the Constitution of the United States aided rather than hindered national expansion. Yet many individual states describe in their constitutions the territorial extent of their sovereignty, as do many Latin-American and European states. And these constitutions have some evidentiary value in boundary disputes before international tribunals. Israel, particularly, is concerned about her boundaries. Her war with her Arab neighbors changed the picture considerably; Israel acquired control of

[1] United States Constitution, Article IV, Sec. 3.

additional territory while losing very little of the area originally intended for her. She also acquired control of New Jerusalem, which was to have become part of an international zone. To serve notice on all the world, therefore, that Israel intends to retain her gains, many of her leaders wanted a bold declaration on the extent of the land over which she asserts sovereignty. Yet, while the boundary situation was so fluid and treaties of peace were not even in the process of negotiation, the Kneset could hardly undertake to fix latitudes and longitudes.

The impassioned debates on boundaries, both within the Committee on the Constitution of the State Council[2] and in the Kneset,[3] did not involve land over which Israel now exercises sovereignty. They involved rather the land over which Jordan exercises sovereignity—the land which the Bible describes as given to the seed of Abraham or the land conquered by Joshua. Herut party spokesmen, in particular, are intolerant of any move that might imply a waiver of Israel's rights to all of erstwhile Palestine and Trans-Jordan.[4] The religious parties concur.

Within the Kneset the divergence of opinion was expressed most fully after the December, 1949, resolution of the United Nations General Assembly regarding the internationalization of Jerusalem. After the approval of this resolution,[5] most of the government offices were moved to Jerusalem and the Kneset convened there on December 26, 1949. In the interim there were reports of negotiations with Jordan for a treaty that would involve the partition of Jerusalem and Israel's recognition of Jordan's sovereignty over the remainder of what once was Palestine. The

[2] *W.H. Proceedings*, Pamphlet I, pp. 6, 21.

[3] These debates in the Kneset were not in connection with any proposed legislation but rather in connection with reports rendered by the Government on foreign affairs, e.g. *Divrei ha-Kneset*, III, 2d Sess., 101st meeting, 375-96.

[4] *W.H. Proceedings*, Pamphlet I, p. 6.

[5] On December 9, 1949. See United Nations General Assembly, Official Records of the Fourth Session, Plenary Meetings, 20 September–10 December, 1949, p. 607.

opposition parties joined in an attack on the coalition Government for the setback which Israel suffered at the United Nations General Assembly sessions and for the rumored peace treaty negotiations with Jordan.[6] The head of the Fighters' Party warned that any compromise on Jerusalem would ultimately lead to a series of capitulations.[7]

The major opposition party—Mapam—with its pro-Soviet orientation, criticized the heavy reliance of the Government upon the friendship of England and the United States in the Jerusalem issue. It also opposed any appeasement of Jordan, which it regarded as a British puppet state whose expansion constituted a gain for British imperialism.[8] Mapam and Herut proposed votes of nonconfidence on the foreign policy of the Israeli Government which were defeated on January 4, 1950.[9] Voting with them, however, were the delegates of the Herut, Fighters', and Communist parties.

The General Zionists did not vote with the opposition, but they too declared their party policy that the proclamation of Jerusalem as the eternal and actual capital of Israel be embodied in the constitution as its first paragraph.[10]

The coalition Government preferred to avoid any legislation or resolutions with regard to boundaries. To mention anything less than the territory described in the Bible would offend the religious parties which agreed with the opposition in principle but voted with the Head of the Government because they were realistic. Constitutional silence, therefore, was deemed the better course.

The problem of Jerusalem and its environs, because of the presence of the Holy Places, is of course complicated beyond the general problem of territorial limitations. When, in 1948, the United Nations failed to provide for the safety of Jerusalem—its inhabitants or its shrines—the Jews, and subsequently the State

[6] *Divrei ha-Kneset*, III, 2d Sess., 101st meeting, 380-94.
[7] *Ibid.*, 102d meeting, 410.
[8] *Ibid.*, 422.
[9] *Ibid.*, 445-446.
[10] *Ibid.*, 446.

of Israel, took over its defense and its relief. To all intents and purposes New Jerusalem became a part of the State. Furthermore, the Security Council had endorsed valid armistice agreements which recognized the control of New Jerusalem by the State of Israel.[11]

Thus it is not likely that Israel would now accept another government for the city, with new courts and new arrangements for public services. Nor would it agree to demilitarization, for "the simultaneous dismissal of Jewish and Arab forces from (the new and old) Jerusalem would not create equal security for both parts of the city. It would put the entire City once more back . . . to the mercy of Arab forces which, by the facts of geography, would then be free to surround it from three sides."[12]

Israel's proposal to the United Nations was that the United Nations limit its commitment to the safeguarding of the Holy Places by initiating such formal agreements with the State of Israel as may be necessary for the implementation of those safeguards.[13] What the United Nations will do can hardly be predicted at this writing. From the point of view of the Israeli constitution, however, it remains to be seen whether Israel will simply give the United Nations rights of extraterritoriality in the Holy Places or consent to their internationalization.

CONSTITUTIONAL PROVISIONS FOR ARMED FORCES

Israel's territorial problems are not constitutionally connected with the problem of the armed forces; it is primarily because of her fear of her neighbors that the latter problem looms so large.

Who shall have the power to declare war and make regulations for an emergency? To what branch of the Government shall the armed forces be attached, and who shall be their commander-in-chief?

These questions were discussed fully by the Committee on the

[11] See A. S. Eban, "Israel and Jerusalem" (Pamphlet 5 of Israeli Office of Information, n.d.), p. 5.

[12] *Ibid.*, p. 7.

[13] *Ibid.*, p. 8.

Constitution of the State Council of the Provisional Government, but no agreement was reached. In 1949, however, the Kneset approved a military service law[14] which indicated what the likely constitutional pattern will be.

The principal issue upon which the parties differed was the conscription of women. To satisfy the Religious Bloc, any woman who, for reasons of religion or conscience, requested exemption was granted it.[15] However, on whether the legislative or the executive authority shall have supreme authority over the army, the divergence of opinion did not reveal party lines.

Dr. Kohn's draft provided for the recruiting and maintenance of the armed forces under the control of the legislature.[16] The president, however, would appoint the commander-in-chief and issue commissions to the officers.[17] Dr. Kohn felt that in a democracy the military establishment must recognize its subservience to the civilian authority.[18] Professor Vitta cautioned that command of the armed forces must rest in the executive.[19] Dr. Wahrhaftig felt that the constitution ought to deal with the military only negatively, to wit: "There shall be no conscription except according to law." Under no circumstances should the military be independent of the legislature. The legislature operates through the Government which may in turn control the army, but in the final analysis, he urged, the legislature should be supreme.[20]

Assuming that the legislature recruits and maintains the military establishment, and assuming further that the legislature declares states of emergency or war, what will happen during periods when the legislature is not in session? Dr. Wahrhaftig had proposed that there be an "interim assembly" which would be in a position to act, but as yet this proposal is not law. Should the Government act on its own? Vitta had suggested in connection with all emergency situations that the Government have the

[14] *Sefer ha-Huqim, 5709*, pp. 271-78.
[15] *Ibid.*, p. 275, sec. 11*d*.
[16] *W.H. Proceedings*, Pamphlet II, Article 46.
[17] *Ibid.*, Article 56.
[18] *Ibid.*, p. 31.
[19] *Ibid.*, Pamphlet V, p. 17.
[20] *Ibid.*, Pamphlet II, pp. 55-56.

power to promulgate regulations to have the effect of law. If the legislature were to fail to enact the regulations into law within thirty days of their promulgation, they would become null and void and the legislature would have to decide the status of legal relations during the interval when the void regulations were in effect.[21] Grabovsky of Mapai felt that the Government should have emergency powers even when the legislature was in session. He argued that the greatest threat to democracy is the inability of the Government to take decisive action in an emergency: parliaments debate while the enemy advances and gets entrenched.[22]

The only proposal on which the majority of the State Council's Committee on the Constitution agreed was the one providing that when a state of emergency shall have been proclaimed in the state by the legislature "the Executive Council shall be permitted to issue emergency regulations which shall have the force of law for a period of three months."[23]

The Kneset resolved only one of these issues. The Minister of Defense was given the power to call persons into military service, but his call was subject to review by the Kneset Committee on Security and Foreign Affairs.[24] Its exemption of women from military service, however, boomeranged. Women were exempt if they certified that they had religious scruples against military service. The result was that most women made the certification.[25] That is why either the exemption had to be withdrawn or some substitute for military service provided, such as service on the farms. After the resignation of the Government in 1951, Ben Gurion sought to have the latter alternative approved by the Kneset.[26] His attempt further antagonized the

[21] *Ibid.*, Pamphlet V, pp. 16, 44.

[22] *Ibid.*, Pamphlet III, p. 47.

[23] *Ibid.*, p. 68.

[24] *Sefer ha-Huqim, 5709*, p. 274, sec. 8.

[25] Though proposed, no exemption was given to any male conscientious objectors. Persons, however, who are not permanently domiciled in Israel may obtain an exemption. *Divrei ha-Kneset*, VIII, 3d Sess., 233rd meeting, 1243-44.

[26] *Ibid.* Ben Gurion was supported by Mapam. See editorial, *'Al-ha-Mishmar*, March 7, 1951, p. 1.

Religious Bloc with Minister of Welfare Lewin, of the Agudat Yisrael, reminding the Kneset that such an amendment to the Military Service Law would be disobeyed by many Jews who would rather be imprisoned or executed.[27]

NATIONALIZATION OF THE ARMY

The nationalization of the army was one problem that was of tremendous importance in the early days of the Provisional Government. Americans may be shocked by this statement, for they cannot visualize how an army can be anything other than the instrument of the state. However, the peculiar development of Israel's armed forces accounts for the unique situation. Years before the mandatory abandoned its civil administration in Palestine, the Jewish colonists found it necessary to seek means for their self-defense. The Haganah was the principal agency.[28] But the Haganah became virtually an underground movement, and other independent underground movements could not be prevented from coming into being. Thus there arose the Irgun Zvai Leumi and the Sternists—each with its own philosophy and program.[29] Even in the Haganah, units developed along party lines so that the Palmach, for example, the best striking force the Jews had, was constituted principally of members of Mapai and Mapam.[30]

During the months of terror before independence, and during the war against the Arabs, it was difficult to coordinate, not to mention consolidate, all the fighting forces. Often the units defeated each other's purposes and sometimes took stern measures against each other. There was even fear of a civil war.

[27] *Divrei ha-Kneset,* VIII, 3d Sess., 233rd meeting, 1250.

[28] For a brief history of the Haganah, see M. Pearlman, *The Army of Israel* (New York, 1950), pp. 12-79.

[29] See J. Borisov, *Palestine Underground* (New York, 1947), pp. 9-23.

[30] D. Winograd, "Tenu'at ha-No'ar ha-'Oved we-ha-Palmah" (The Labor Youth Movement and the Palmach) *ha-Ma'aleh,* June 14, 1938, p. 216.

One of Ben Gurion's first orders[31] established the Defense Army of Israel, with an all-out mandate for consolidation. His order was ultimately fulfilled, but not before the Atalena incident and the assassination of the United Nations mediator, which focused world-wide attention on the problem.

Mapam had sought to include in the compulsory military service law a provision that military units might be organized along the lines of collective settlements, which would enable Mapam to control the units organized from members of its own settlements.[32] The proposal was defeated, though trainees were permitted to retain their status in their qibuzim. Ben Gurion's order, however, is still in effect and the maintenance of any armed force outside the Defense Army of Israel is forbidden.[33]

[31] *'Iton Rishmi,* May 31, 1948, p. 10.

[32] *Divrei ha-Kneset,* II, 1st Sess., 79th meeting, 1613. Mapam's desire to control part of the army was criticized in an editorial, "Zavah u-Miflagot" (Army and Parties), *be-Terem,* 7 Iyar, 5708: May 15, 1948, pp. 3-5.

[33] Section 4 of the ordinance, *'Iton Rishmi,* May 31st, 1948. Supp. 1, p. 9.

CHAPTER XI

The Status of Non-Israeli Jews

THEIR RIGHT TO EMIGRATE

The oneness of the Jewish people—those in Israel and those outside—is not only a dogma of the Jewish faith but also a tenet of political Zionism. Even Zionists committed to an altogether secularist conception of their movement, including many whose views are Marxist in character, agree on this point. The State of Israel, therefore, is regarded by virtually every Jew residing in Israel as partly responsible for the welfare and future of Jewish communities throughout the world. Moreover, the State of Israel is too much in need of the moral and financial support of Jews in some countries to ignore their will. Thus there arise some limitations on its autonomy which are at least *de facto,* if not *de jure.* For that reason one writer expressed herself as follows: "Autonomy is not the proper term of reference for defining Israel's status vis-à-vis the Diaspora and the Diaspora's relationship to Israel."[1]

The constitutional problems that arise from this situation can be divided into those pertaining to the rights of individual Jews outside of Israel and those pertaining to a world-wide organization of non-Israeli Jews. And all of these have received a considerable amount of attention.

It was anticipated by the Committee on the Constitution of the State Council of the Provisional Government that every Jew

[1] Trude Weiss Rosmarin, "Israel and the Diaspora," *Jewish Spectator,* XIV, No. 11 (October 1949), 5.

in the world would have a right to emigrate to Israel. As has already been pointed out, the proposals ranged from an unlimited right, including the granting of citizenship to stateless Jews wherever they may be and whenever they may become such, to the granting of the right to only those who indicate their readiness to emigrate immediately.[2]

It was this section that contained what Professor M. R. Konvitz called the "open-door-for-Jews policy," and he questioned its wisdom or discretion.[3]

Since the article would not be self-enforcing, Konvitz felt that no Jew outside of Israel could win enforcement of his right of admission should the government of Israel refuse to let him in, "for no constitution vests rights in a foreigner outside of the state's territory." He cited no authorities and one has reason to wonder why a Jewish immigrant, at a point of debarkation in Israel, could not avail himself of such an article of the constitution to challenge, for example, a statute which went beyond providing what Dr. Kohn calls "rules of order." What really troubled Professor Konvitz was the uncomplimentary comparison with Nazi Germany, which claimed the right of intervention on behalf of Germans in the Sudetenland. Furthermore, he felt that the article embodied a principle of exclusion which constitutes religious discrimination. Jews will enjoy the right; non-Jews will not enjoy it. Until the DP camps had been liquidated this was reasonable, but thereafter it would be inconsistent with democratic policy: "It may be difficult to explain, after the DP's are provided for, that a policy for Jews is justifiable by the tests of a broad democratic philosophy, while a policy of America for white Protestants is not justifiable."[4]

Even from Konvitz's point of view, it might have been possi-

[2] See *supra,* pp. 39-40.

[3] M. Konvitz, "The Bill of Rights in the Draft Constitution for Israel," *The Reconstructionist,* XIV, No. 20 (February 4, 1949), 11-12.

[4] *Ibid.*

ble to fulfill the underlying intention of the article—to give persecuted Jews a right of admission—if it provided a right of asylum to all persecutees as set forth in Article 14 of the Universal Declaration of Human Rights of the General Assembly of the United Nations. Special mention might be made of the fact that historical considerations prompt Israel to make this right available especially to Jews. Their right to asylum would be assured not only in the event of political persecution but also in the event of the refusal of a country of origin to permit them to conserve their own culture, as in the case of the USSR. It should not be difficult to justify this exception in a country where citizenship has been, and still is, based on *ius sanguinis*. When citizenship is based on *ius sanguinis,* cultural considerations, as well as blood relationships, come into play and do not offend against principles of international law. By the same token, one persecuted because of his desire to conserve a Hebraic culture in the country of his origin might have a special right of asylum in a country where that culture prevails. In the event of persecution for political reasons, however, the right should be without discrimination.

The First Kneset did approve a law[5] which gave Jews everywhere an unlimited right to emigrate to Israel, unless they are enemies of the Jewish people or would endanger health or security.

THE DEFINITION OF A "JEW"

Another question that could not easily be resolved was "Who is a Jew?"[6] Would all religious sects in the world that claim they are Jews enjoy the right? And in the event that a Jew had married a non-Jew, what would be the status of the non-Jewish spouse seeking an immigrant's visa? Presently the religious courts would resolve the issue by Jewish canon law. And a number of

[5] See *Divrei ha-Kneset,* VI, 2d Sess., 160th meeting, 2035-40 and 2041-48; *ibid.,* 162nd meeting, 2088 and 2094-2107; and *Sefer ha-Huqim, 5710,* p. 159.

[6] See *Sheluhot,* 25 Tishrei, 5711: October 6, 1950, pp. 6-8.

such cases have been thus resolved. But there are persons who were persecuted in Germany as Jews, and yet, from the point of view of Judaism, would not qualify as such. The child of a non-Jewish mother by a Jewish father is not a Jew according to Judaism, though in Nazi Germany he was so regarded. As a matter of fact, the same would apply to many persons recognized by Liberal Judaism the world over as Jews who would yet be non-Jews by the law of Israel's Rabbinic courts. This is one of the difficult legal problems involved in the granting of rights to Jews extraterritorially.

The problem of the right of non-Jewish spouses of Jews to emigrate to Israel has received world-wide attention. The Israel Foreign Office denied a report by the American Religious News Service which gave the impression that non-Jews who marry Jews must be converted to Judaism in order to remain in Israel. Its statement said:

> There is no basis for the report that non-Jews married to Jews must be converted in order to live in Israel. Every Jew desiring to emigrate to Israel is regarded as a returning resident, according to the open door policy of the state of Israel. The applications of all others are considered on their merits, and non-Jews must qualify under the immigration ordinance. The fact is that many non-Jews, including the partners of mixed marriages, have been admitted. Conversion is never required as a condition of admittance.[7]

The truth, however, is that if the non-Jewish spouse is converted to Judaism, her right to admission is forthwith conceded. This may be a species of "coercion."

With regard to citizenship also Jews may enjoy an advantage. The Government proposed a bill[8] that any Jew immigrating to Israel to settle there shall automatically become a citizen and even have the privilege of retaining the citizenship of his country of origin. This was done to enable immigrants to hold on to

[7] Jewish Telegraphic Agency, *Daily News Bulletin* (New York), XVII, No. 71 (April 13, 1950), 2.

[8] *Reshumot, Haza'ot Hok*, No. 48, 12 Tammuz, 5710, pp. 190-94.

whatever advantages their earlier citizenship would afford with regard to property rights in the country from whence they came. The bill was still under consideration at the expiration of the First Kneset.

THE PROBLEM OF THE JEWISH AGENCY

The relationship between the Jewish Agency and the State of Israel was the subject of a prolonged controversy. Mapai was the strongest party in Israel. In the World Zionist Organization, on the other hand, the General Zionists, with their principal strength in the United States, constituted the largest party. Since the World Zionist Organization dominates the Agency, Mapai did not relish the thought of giving the Agency special status vis-à-vis the State. Furthermore, the principal function of the Agency—to support immigration to Israel—was regarded as the "chief purpose and function of the State itself."[9] For the State to delegate this function to another body might be tantamount to a mitigation of its sovereignty. The General Zionists, in turn, did not relish the thought of the State's control of the Agency's funds and the State's usurpation of all of the Agency's functions. They would have liked to see the Zionist Organization become "the representative of World Jewry—expressing their collective will to complete the task of national rehabilitation in Israel and the spiritual and cultural renaissance of the Jewish people as a whole."[10]

The General Zionists defended their position on the theory that unless the Agency was autonomous, American Jews could not participate in it. If the Agency was an organ of the State of Israel, American Jews would have involved themselves in charges that they were active in a foreign state. The Laborites countered

[9] Bulletin of the Israel Office of Information, "Four Years of Israel's Statehood: The Story of Immigration" (R P 17/A-April, 1952), p. 1.

[10] E. Neumann, "The Zionist Movement and the State of Israel," *Jewish Mail*, III, No. 16 (April 25, 1952), 5.

with the argument that participation in the relief and rehabilitation work of an Agency, under the control of another state, was not disloyalty to America—or "dual allegiance"—any more than participation in the International Red Cross would be.

The World Zionist Congress considered the problem during its sessions in August, 1951. If it is to be resolved at all, however, it will be in cooperation with the Second Kneset, not the First.

CHAPTER XII

Economic and Social Problems[1]

FOREIGN CAPITAL AND THE INVESTMENT LAW

Capital is the key to Israel's economic future. She may not become a great producer of basic raw materials. However, she does have an abundant supply of skilled manpower.[2] Yet, to provide employment for all would require at least $500,000,000 of investment capital.[3] To attract these millions from foreign sources the Government made certain concessions. Prospective investors charged that there ought to be constitutional guarantees that successful enterprises will not some day be taken over by the state, though the payment of compensation was assured by the First Kneset's Fundamental Principles. Furthermore, because of the unique character of Israel's federation of labor, the Histadrut, which itself owns a vast network of industries, new industrialists were apprehensive that the strike might become an instrument to force the sale of an enterprise to the very union with which a dis-

[1] For a good brief description of Israel's social order (for Jews) by a member of the Kneset, see Eli'ezer Liebenstein, "Israel's Social Order," *Congress Weekly*, XVII, No. 15 (April 24, 1950), 4-6.

[2] It was estimated that 58 percent of the population consists of persons between the ages of fifteen and fifty, the ages of peak employability (*Shenaton ha-Memshalah, 5710*, p. 214).

[3] For a brief summary of Israel's economic problems and some proposed solutions, see A. Dickenstein, "Israel's Economic Problems," *Jewish Frontier*, XVII, No. 7 (July, 1950), 14-17. Also John Stephens, "Israel's Economic Progress," *Foreign Commerce Weekly*, XL, No. 13 (September 1950), 3-6.

pute arose. The Histadrut, whose leaders were in the Government and whose membership constituted the principal source of Mapai's strength, always had the Government on its side. It thus enjoyed advantages over competing private businesses. It was for this reason that the Government was criticized by the Herut party and the General Zionists.[4]

The Government countered with the argument that Israel had a planned economy. Investors who were prepared to develop an industry which enjoyed a high priority according to the Government's plan, were given full cooperation. Investors who simply wanted to compete with existing industries made no substantial contribution to the economy, for, in a country where profits were rigidly controlled, prices were kept low without competition. Competition might have helped to increase efficiency in production, but national enthusiasm was so great that efficiency was promoted considerably by ideological factors alone. That was why, when there was a choice between a new industry—of which there was almost unlimited need—and a competing industry, the Government favored the former.

On March 29, 1950, the Kneset approved of an investment law[5] which has great constitutional significance. To enjoy the advantages of the provisions of the law, the undertaking had to be one of those approved by the Government's investment center (sec. 1). Machinery, plants, and raw materials required for such undertakings were exempted from import duties (sec. 24). For at least five years and sometimes, on application, for an added five years, new buildings or additions to existing buildings, to house the approved undertakings, were exempt from property taxes (secs. 3 and 4). The allowances for depreciation were 200

[4] An excellent summary of the principal arguments of Mapai and the General Zionists is given in H. Lehrman, *Israel: The Beginning and Tomorrow* (New York, 1951), pp. 158-78.

[5] *Divrei ha-Kneset*, III, 2d Sess., 7th meeting, 325-29, 334-43, 347-66; *ibid.*, 9th meeting, 451-74; *ibid.*, IV, 20th meeting, 1211-30; and *Sefer ha-Huqim, 5710*, pp. 129-36.

percent of normal rates for the first three years, and 150 percent for the following two years, with discretion to add another 50 percent of normal rates in case of unusual wear and tear (sec. 10). Capital expenditures for scientific research could be amortized over a five-year period (sec. 16). For the first five years, income from an approved undertaking was subject to a maximum tax of 25 percent (sec. 11). When foreign companies paid taxes in Israel which exceeded the deductions allowable in the home country, Israel would refund the difference (sec. 12).[6] Withdrawals from Israel in the currency of the original investment on account of the capital, profits and interest from, or depreciation of the investment, were permitted to a maximum of 10 percent per annum of the investment (sec. 21). While a special body known as the "Investment Center" was created to determine what were approved undertakings, an applicant had the right to appeal to the Minister of Finance and the Minister of Trade and Industry (sec. 29).

The Government endeavored to attract foreign capital and to quash rumors that capitalist enterprise had no chance in Israel. The Head of the Government, while a Laborite, was not committed to any doctrinaire socialist views.[7] His principal goal was his country's general welfare and economic development.

[6] Some of the income tax exemptions apply also to "specialists" who come to Israel to improve its technical processes (sec. 13).

[7] Some of the Mapam Qibuzim refused to hire day laborers from among the new immigrants since that would have involved the payment of daily wages. The "Qibuzniks" themselves do not take wages and they invite immigrants to join them on the basis of equality. They decline, however, to become employers. Ben Gurion objected to their blind adherence to an ideal which was only hampering the economic absorption and training of their newly arrived brethren. However, he had no power to coerce the hiring of labor. Nonetheless, his opposition to doctrinaire socialism was demonstrated again. The doctrinaire position of the Socialist Mapam and the nondoctrinaire position of the Socialist Mapai are also clearly reflected in their attitudes toward loans from foreign countries. Mapam opposed loans from western countries, and none were forthcoming from the east. Mapai accepted loans and goods from the former, and perhaps would have accepted them from the latter, too—if they had been offered.

Mapai also favors the lowering of wages as the cost of living is lowered. Mapam has tried to make political capital of this and has threatened "go-

Agreements were also made with foreign corporations, permitting a limited withdrawal in foreign currency each year. This was discrimination in favor of *nonresidents*, as were many provisions of the investment law, and therefore did not violate the Fundamental Principles of the Kneset which called for nondiscrimination among *residents*. However, there was insistence that large blocks of stock in some of the investing corporations be made available to Israelis or to the Government.[8]

The constitutional problem presented by the Government's program for greater industrialization was not one of constitutional power, as it might have been in the United States. It was rather the inadequacy of administration. It was this evil that Yaacov Geri, as Minister of Trade, endeavored to correct.

AGRICULTURE AND HOUSING

A constitutional problem may emerge with regard to agriculture. It was conceded that private farming was not too practical and only cooperative or collectivist farming could succeed. However, the percentage of the population engaged in farming was hardly adequate.[9] The Government therefore offered inducements to immigrants to engage in it. For that reason also Mapai organized volunteer units to devote themselves to the land. However, it was assumed by the Government that it could conscript persons for the purpose.[10] The suggestion that women, who are

---

slow" tactics in production, though all recognize that increased production is the only way to balance the export-import ratio to enable the country to increase its absorptive capacity. See *Zion* (November, 1949), pp. 5-7.

[8] The agreement with the Palestine Potash Corporation provides for an option to the Government to purchase all the stock on one year's notice.

[9] P. Bernard Nortman, "Planning Israel's Economic Future," *Jewish Horizon*, XII, No. 7 (March, 1950), 9-10. Also *Shenaton ha-Memshalah, 5710*, p. 20. Thus far less than 10 percent of the total land available is under cultivation.

[10] The reclamation, utilization, and cultivation of the land pertains also to defense and not only to food supply (*Shenaton ha-Memshalah, 5710*, p. 19). Conscription for this purpose, therefore, might present no constitutional problem even in the United States.

exempt from military service, be conscripted for farming created the issue already discussed herein.[11] Yet it is significant that the objection was to the conscription of *women,* not conscription for farming.

The housing shortage, which was acute, was partly relieved by the Government by actual construction on its part as well as by construction financed jointly with private investment companies. The only constitutional problem that is suggested pertains to the land on which much of this construction work was done and on which many agricultural communities were being founded. The Government became the custodian of abandoned Arab property. Hundreds of thousands of these acres were sold to the Jewish National Fund and other groups. When this land is ultimately sought by its Arab owners, it remains to be seen how many will be regarded as enemy aliens and how many as citizens who are entitled to compensation.

The extent of Israel's caution with regard to expropriation can be gleaned from the fact that it did not confiscate the British oil refineries at Haifa, though conversations with an attorney who saw the old agreements between the mandatory and the companies revealed how unconscionable they were. They provided for the exemption of the companies from all existing and future taxes and customs. The companies were also given free use of water and building materials as well as the right to expropriate needed land, to import labor without immigration restrictions, and to build harbors, railroads, airports, and radio stations without any control by the government. Furthermore, during Israel's war the refineries had sold their oil to the Arabs.

Nonetheless, it appears that to protect the rights of organized labor, the Government did exercise even "coercion." On May 23, 1950, on the occasion of picketing by union agricultural workers against citrus fruit growers who hired cheap immigrant labor, the Minister of Labor, Golda Meyerson, said that such growers

[11] See *supra,* pp. 151-52.

would not receive state aid if a single worker were found in their groves whose employment did not come about through established channels.[12]

THE SOCIAL PROBLEM

Israel's social problems did not create any major constitutional issues. The immigrants came from diverse lands and cultures and to create national unity was a herculean task. Language was one instrument for the fulfillment of this goal, and a supreme effort was being made to have everyone speak Hebrew. Arabic, it appears, was becoming less important, since the Arab population was hardly 15 percent of the total. However, as was already noted, Mapam wanted Arabic to enjoy a special status by the very terms of the constitution.[13]

More serious than the language problem, however, was the problem of the mores. As has already been noted,[14] child marriages were outlawed. Education for girls became compulsory, despite the objection of oriental Jews.

The new immigrants from oriental countries, in the main, were unfamiliar with modern requirements of health and sanitation. The Government had to educate them in these matters. Occasionally there was resentment, but no one doubted that the Government would be empowered to do anything called for by the situation.

The more serious problem was the amalgamation of all the diverse groups into a homogeneous nation. With settlements being made by persons with the same cultural background this aim was being defeated rather than advanced. That is why there were attempts at mixed Qibuzim such as Sa'ad, whose pioneers were half Yemenite and half European. The Government was also aware of a racial problem. Many of the oriental Jews are as

[12] *Divrei ha-Kneset,* V, 2d Sess., 142nd meeting, 1450.
[13] See *supra,* p. 43. [14] See *supra,* p. 134.

dark as Negroes, and intermarriages had to be encouraged to prevent any possible cleavage between white and black Jews.[15]

The North African Jews were even more of a problem than the sturdy, intelligent, industrious Yemenites, who endeared themselves to the earlier settlers. The North African Jews were incredibly superstitious. Even the spokesmen of the Religious Bloc hardly cared to call them "religious." They were so truly primitive that their traditional observances bordered on the pagan. They have presented no special constitutional problem but one wonders how long it will take for them to mature politically.

Israel also has non-Jewish minorities. In addition to the Muslim and Christian Arabs, there are small groups of religious and national minorities such as Druzes, Circassians, Armenians, Bahais, and Parsis.[16] The war had created a great upheaval in the social and economic life of almost all these groups. Many of their villages were destroyed with most of their agricultural equipment. Those who lived in the urban centers were in many cases deprived of the whole basis of their material existence.[17] Their earlier social and political organization also vanished. To reintegrate this non-Jewish population into the new economic and social structure was the avowed responsibility of the First Kneset.[18] The Government granted subventions and loans to promote their farming. It tried to find employment for those Arab urban residents who were once government clerks, as well as for those whose economic existence was previously based on the presence of a neighboring populous Arab community. The Histadrut also supported the growth of an Arab cooperative movement. Furthermore, the Government trained Arab personnel for teaching and social welfare work.

[15] Y. Adelstein, "le-Mizug ha-Galuyot be-Yisrael" (The Merger of the Exiles in Israel), *Sheluhot*, No. 27, 25 Tammuz, 5711: July 29, 1951, p. 7.

[16] See I. Ben-Zevi, "Minorities in Israel," *Zion*, November, 1949, pp. 12-16.

[17] D. R. Elston, "Arabs in Israel," *Israel and Middle East*, III (January–March, 1951), 13.

[18] *Ibid.*, pp. 16-25.

From a constitutional point of view, it can be said that the situation of these non-Jews was neither that of politically integrated citizens nor that of national or ethnic minorities but rather a mixture of both. In the Communist party they were integrated. In the 1951 elections Mapam had Arabs on their list of candidates, one of whom (a Christian) was elected. Mapai, on the other hand, sponsored separate lists for them. Arabic was not an official second language but the official gazette appeared in Arabic as well as Hebrew. Coins, postage stamps, and banknotes also bore Arabic inscriptions. Arabic was also the medium of instruction in all state-maintained schools for these minorities. It is likely that the pattern of the future will depend not only upon social developments within Israel, but also upon the character of Israel's relationships with her neighboring Arab states.

Cultural activity in Israel was very high. And culture too was a Government responsibility. The Ministry of Education and Culture, in its Department of Culture, had a section for the promotion of literature and art, with subsections for literature, science, music, plastic arts, drama and dance, folklore, and national celebrations.[19]

There was a dearth of schools for secondary and higher education, but these too were being established rapidly. Generally it may be said that the Government saw but one limitation on its powers with regard to social and economic development—its finances. Constitutionally speaking, however, the limitations were nil.

POLYGAMY AND CAPITAL PUNISHMENT

The two social problems, however, which required resolution and which challenged the Government's dedication to the principle of equality for males and females, Arabs and Jews, were polygamy and capital punishment. With regard to polygamy all the difficulties encountered with regard to the abolition of child

[19] *Shenaton ha-Memshalah, 5710,* p. 99

marriages were met anew, though finally overcome.[20] Capital punishment, however, which Judaism virtually outlawed two millenia ago, was regarded as a "must" for Arabs. If the State did not practice it then the family of a murdered Arab would itself pursue the "blood-feud" against the murderer. Israel's Minister of Police was firm in his opposition to the abolition of capital punishment, though this was one issue with regard to which even Mapam and the Religious Bloc were agreed.[21]

The law proposed in the Kneset for the abolition of capital punishment excepted traitors.[22] To this exception the leader of the Communist party objected.[23] He feared that the Government itself, presumably if it supported American warmongering, might be committing the treason and would have to be killed to save the people. Mapai's spokesmen were divided on the entire issue. Many felt that moral values were not yet secure enough in the world to permit the abolition of the death penalty.[24]

[20] See *supra*, p. 134.
[21] *Divrei ha-Kneset*, VI, 2d Sess., 169th meeting, 2302-2304.
[22] *Reshumot, Haza'ot Hok*, July 10, 1949, No. 15, p. 159.
[23] *Divrei ha-Kneset*, VI, 2d Sess., 169th meeting, 2291.
[24] For an English summary of the debate see the *Jewish Frontier*, XVII, No. 11 (November 1950), 6-9.

CHAPTER XIII

The Outlook for the Future

DEMOCRATIC CHARACTER OF THE CONSTITUTION

The character of Israel's constitution was very much predetermined by the Kneset Israel, out of which the state emerged organically, and it is likely that the State will continue indefinitely to have a parliamentary form of government similar to that of the Kneset Israel. However, the legislature almost forthwith became but a brake on the executive branch and one finds no evidence whatever of a growing initiative on the part of the legislators to assume leadership in the lawmaking process. If the parties become fewer in number it may happen that one of them will have a majority in the Kneset. The Government will then consist of the leaders of that party and its legislative and executive power will be virtually unlimited except for such criticism as will come from the opposition parties and public opinion. Since the courts have no power of judicial review and constitutional limitations are nil, the democratic character of the State may be in jeopardy.

Nonetheless, most Israelis are not concerned. They believe that the ultimate preservation of democratic institutions depends less upon constitutional guarantees than upon the general consensus of the land's inhabitants. In the Kneset debate on the constitution it was said[1] that the written constitutions of many

[1] *Divrei ha-Kneset,* IV, 2d Sess., 113th meeting, 725-26.

European and Latin-American states contained eloquently democratic provisions while basic human rights and fundamental freedoms in these states simply did not exist—as Jews well knew.

The future, however, will reveal whether Israel can maintain the freedom of her citizens—comparable to that now prevailing in the western democracies—even while her economy is a planned one like that of socialist states. This synthesis Israel has sought to achieve even as she has tried to be neutral in the cold war between East and West.

Success with such a synthesis may not be too meaningful to the world at large. At best Israel may some day have five or ten million citizens. Her population will hardly be as large as that of New York city alone. And even if they continue to enjoy full civil and political freedom in a planned economy, the pattern is not likely to be applicable to countries with hundreds of millions of inhabitants spread over millions of square miles. Furthermore, for at least a few decades longer Israel will have to engage in the absorption of mostly penniless immigrants to whom even subsistence living represents an improvement over what they had before. There will be no bloody resistance, as the United States might anticipate, to any change from free capitalist enterprise to socialism. Israel has no problem even comparable to the Soviets' declassing of certain elements in society.

Nonetheless, for Israel to develop this synthesis, peace in the Middle East is necessary. And it is therefore not respect for Jewish tradition alone that has given the historic Jewish salutation, "Shalom" (meaning peace), its new vibrancy and significance. Furthermore, Israel will require much capital and herculean efforts to be expended in the direction of promoting social homoegeneity. This is well known. However, the more relevant question here is: What constitutional changes were indicated as desiderata after three years of independence?

THE PROBLEM OF NUMEROUS PARTIES

Most of the faults found with Israel's constitution are due to the multiplicity of political parties, the mutual hostility and suspicion of the parties, and the perpetual domination of the parties by their leaders.

Since elections for the Kneset were on a countrywide basis, even the small parties usually had a chance to elect one or more candidates. Thereby the party leaders could prolong their control. They headed the tickets of their parties, and position on these tickets was, of course, tremendously important. Those who headed the ticket ran only a small risk of losing in a national election, while they might have been defeated if they had had to run in a small electoral district. They could also reward the faithful within the party with a better position on the national list.

Unless a way is found to reduce the number of parties, party political activity will continue to be more important to most of the legislators than lawmaking and law enforcement. Much of the physical and intellectual resources now expended to protect the party's interests in the Kneset and the Government, as well as in the parliamentary and the interministerial committees, could then be dedicated to the over-all welfare of the state, the development of greater expertness in limited areas, and the general political education of the masses, without excessive party rancor that only aggravates the disunity in an already dangerously heterogeneous society.

The perpetuation of the control of the party heads over their organizations has tended to perpetuate the feuding over ideologies even when circumstances have so changed that historic conflicts have become anachronistic. Agudat Yisrael, for example, still agitates for its own school system with little or no instruction in anything but Torah, despite the fact that it recognizes the need for trained personnel in science, engineering, and political administration. As a matter of fact it wants its own party members to obtain skills in these areas for government service. But the preservation of its own school system is necessary for party purposes, and it will not take account of the change in circumstances to sacrifice an immediate party advantage for a more universal good which will also ultimately contribute to the fulfillment of the party's own ideology.

By the same token, the secularists' persistent attacks on the religious parties with the use of the epithet "clericalism" would prompt one to believe that the religious parties in Israel possessed the wealth that churches had in Europe when revolutionaries felt impelled to expropriate them as a prerequisite to economic reform. The religious parties in Israel have the least amount of economic power, and the membership of Agudat Yisrael in particular consists in the main of persons who are wards of charity. Nonetheless, the secularists fanned the flames of hostility and described how Ben Gurion was the captive of bearded tycoons.

That party hostility should so distort the perspective of the leaders is regrettable because Mapai and ha-Po'el ha-Mizrahi are divided principally on the religious issue. Since ha-Po'el ha-Mizrahi is the lion partner in the United Religious Bloc,[2] its merger with Mapai on a common economic, social, and political program would almost give them a majority of all the votes in the country. And one large faction of ha-Po'el ha-Mizrahi seeks such a merger. With Mapai becoming more oriented to the West than to the East, and with the cleavage between itself and Mapam becoming more pronounced, the Progressives could also join Mapai without too great an ideological compromise. Despite the fact that the weight of General Zionist opinion the world over wants the Progressives and the General Zionists in Israel to merge, the General Zionists in Israel have more in common, from an eco-

[2] In the 1951 elections to the Kneset, it won eight seats while the other three religious parties together won a total of seven.

nomic point of view, with the Herut and Mizrahi parties than with the Progressives.

THE RELIGIOUS ISSUE

Even on the religious issue, which is still the principal problem delaying the drafting of a written constitution, the religious parties are neither united nor even notably respectful of each other's points of view. During the debate in the Kneset on the constitution they gave the appearance of unity. But the unity was not real.

The Religious Bloc abstained as a group from voting on the resolution finally approved. But on another resolution[3]—very similar in content—the Mizrahi and ha-Po'el ha-Mizrahi had instructed party members that they could vote as they pleased. It was the rabbis of the Agudat Yisrael who had ruled, as a matter of religious law, that there should be no written constitution other than the Torah. Agudat Yisrael's representatives in the Kneset felt bound by this ruling. The Mizrahi and ha-Po'el ha-Mizrahi, who were generally more progressive than Agudat Yisrael in religious matters, were not so bound. On the final vote all abstained from voting instead of showing a cleavage within the ranks of the religionists.[4] But it remains to be seen what they will do if, and when, chapters of the constitution are proposed in accordance with the Kneset resolution on the constitution.

However, the basic differences between the Mizrahi and Agudat Yisrael groups will emerge with respect to all Jewish law. The former are much more reconciled than the latter to further Jewish legal development so that a greater equality between males and females may be achieved. The former have even been urging the Chief Rabbinate to accelerate such progress while the latter have constantly stayed action by the Chief Rabbinate

[3] This was known as the Kesseh proposal and was submitted at a meeting of the Government. See *ha-Arez*, 32nd year, June 14, 1950, p. 1.
[4] *Ibid.*

and even created their own rabbinic authority as a threat to the already constituted body. The Minister of Religions, Rabbi J. L. Maimon of Mizrahi, made an attempt to force a rabbinical conference to consider the convocation of a Sanhedrin which might make some changes in Jewish law. But again, with objections principally from the Agudat Yisrael, his attempt aborted.[5]

Fundamentalists know how to frighten most of the faithful into submission. That is why Mizrahi and ha-Po'el ha-Mizrahi have usually submitted to the much smaller intransigent Agudat Yisrael and permitted the latter to be as obstructionist as it has been. Agudat Yisrael was less respectful of Mizrahi when it insisted on its own religious school system independently of the Mizrahi system. The differences between the two groups of religious parties have prompted cynics to say that there must be two Torahs, since each of the two groups has its own distinctive approach. In the Second Kneset the cleavage became so great that the parties virtually warred on each other on the trivial issue of the conscription of women for labor. The result has been benign for neither and certainly not for the creation of a closer understanding between left and right in the country as a whole.

ADDED DESIDERATA

The resolution of the religious issue would clear the way for the drafting of a written constitution and the possible merger of Mapai with the religious labor parties. Economic programs and philosophies would then remain as the principal causes for party division. The parties would divide on the basis of their distance to the right or left of center. Such a situation would be healthy for the state, and if there were to be a change from national elections to district elections, there would be an additional stimulus to the fusion of parties.

[5] He has published a volume on the subject, entitled *Hidush ha-Sanhedrin be-Medinateinu ha-Mehudeshet* (The Revival of the Sanhedrin in Our Revived State) (Jerusalem, 5711).

The change from national elections to district elections would also affect the character of municipal elections. Heretofore, the parties in municipal elections were the same as in the national elections and the issues were national issues. In municipal administration there also had to be coalition governments, which did not make for the most efficient results.

District elections would afford constituents the opportunity of having direct contact with their own representatives. The party leaders would also face an electorate in a limited area and not be as certain of election as they now are when they head a national slate.

Another desideratum would be greater decentralization of administration with better trained civil servants. This would help particularly to achieve the aims of the investments law of 1950.[6]

Israel will yet see constitutional development. However, it is difficult to avoid the conclusion that the principal patterns of its constitution were already formed in the first three years of the State's existence. The principal changes of the future will most likely be found in party organization and practices.

[6] See *supra*, p. 163.

Bibliography

OFFICIAL SOURCES

GOVERNMENT OF ISRAEL

Divrei ha-Kneset (The Kneset Record). 9 vols. Jerusalem, 1949–51.

Gilyon Minhelet ha-'Am, Zawim we-Hoda'ot (Bulletin of the Minhelet ha-'Am, Orders and Proclamations). Tel Aviv, 1948.

Government Yearbooks, 5711, 5712. Jerusalem, 1950–51.

Israel Consulate. Political Parties in Israel. Mimeographed. November 15, 1948.

Israel Office of Information. The Arabs in Israel. January, 1952.

———. Israel and Jerusalem. By A. S. Eban. Pamphlet No. 5, n.d.

'Iton Rishmi (Official Gazette). Tel Aviv, 1948–49.

Ozar Pisqei Din (Treasury of Judgments). Jerusalem, 1950.

Proceedings, Mo'ezet ha-'Am (People's Council) and Mo'ezet ha-Medinah ha-Zemanit (Provisional State Council). 2 vols. Tel Aviv, 1948–49.

Proceedings, Wa'adat ha-Huqah (Committee on the Constitution). 5 pamphlets. Ha-Qiryah, 1949.

Qovez ha-Taqanot (Collection of Regulations). 3 vols. Jerusalem, 1949–51.

Reshumot, Haza'ot Hok (Records: Proposed Bills). 3 vols. Jerusalem, 1949–51.

Sefer ha-Huqim (The Book of Laws). 3 vols. Jerusalem, 1949–51.

Shenaton ha-Memshalah (Government Yearbook), 5709, 5710, 5711. Jerusalem, 1948–50.

PALESTINE GOVERNMENT

Laws of Palestine. R. H. Drayton, ed. 2 vols. London: Waterlow & Sons, Ltd., 1934.

Legislation of Palestine, 1918–1925. Compiled by N. Bentwich, Attorney General. 2 vols. Jerusalem, 1926.

Official Gazette of the Government of Palestine. 1920–32.
Palestine Gazette. 1932–38.
Palestine Law Reports.
Survey of Palestine. 1946.

UNITED NATIONS

Official Records of the Fourth Session of the General Assembly. Plenary meetings. Lake Success, 1949.
Official Records of the Second Session of the General Assembly. Resolutions (A/519). Lake Success, 1948.
Report of Palestine Commission to the General Assembly (A/532). Lake Success, 1948.
Summary Record of Proceedings of Palestine Commission (A/AC.-21/SRI-75). Unpublished.

NONOFFICIAL SOURCES

Adelstein, Y. "Le-Mizug ha-Galuyot be'Yisrael" (The Intermarriage of Exiles in Israel), *Sheluhot* (Jerusalem), No. 27 (25 Tammuz, 5711: July 29, 1951).
Agudat Yisrael. She'arim. Special Supplement, June 29, 1950.
American Jewish Congress. Memorandum of Russian Lawyers on Proposed Israeli Constitution. Mimeographed. 1948.
Arad, S. "Israel and the United Nations," *Jewish Frontier* (New York), Vol. XVIII, No. 4 (April, 1950).
Assaf, M. "The Non-Jewish Population of Israel," *Israel* (Tel Aviv: Ichud 'Olami), January, 1950.
Attias, M. Kneset Yisrael be'Erez Yisrael (The Kneset Israel in the Land of Israel). Jerusalem: Wa'ad Leumi, 1944.
Avner, Meir. "Al ha-Haza'ah bi-Dvar ha-Behirot le-Veit ha Nivharim" (On the Proposal with Respect to the Elections to the Assembly), *ha-Arez* (Tel Aviv), 12 Tishrei, 5709: October 15, 1948.
Bar-Ilan, M. "Taskir" (Memorandum), *Yavneh* (Jerusalem), Vol. III, Nisan, 5709: April, 1949.
Baron, Salo W. Social and Religious History of the Jews. 3 vols. New York: Columbia University Press, 1937.
Bar-Shirah, Y. "Mi-Bayoteha Shel Parlamentariyut Yisraelit" (On the Issues of Israeli Parliamentarianism), *Molad* (Tel Aviv), No. 11 (Shevat, 5709: February, 1949).

Ben Gurion, David. "Le-Yisud ha-Medinah" (On the Establishment of the State), *Ha-Po'el ha-Za'ir* (Tel Aviv), Vol. XIV, No. 13, 1948.

Ben-Zevi, I. "Minorities in Israel," *Zion* (Jerusalem), November, 1949.

Bickerman, Elias J. "Historical Foundations of Post-Biblical Judaism," in The Jews: Their History, Culture and Religion, L. Finkelstein, ed. 4 vols. Philadelphia: Jewish Pub. Soc., Vol. I, 1949.

Bilby, K. New Star in the Near East. New York: Doubleday, 1951.

Blanshard, Paul. "Israel: Church and State," *The Nation* (New York), Vol. 170, No. 21 (May 27, 1950).

Borisov, J. Palestine Underground. New York: Judea Pub. Co., 1947.

Burstein, M. Self-Government of the Jews in Palestine. Tel Aviv: Hapoel Hazair, 1934.

Davis, H. M. Constitutions, Electoral Laws, Treaties of States in the Near and Middle East. Durham, N. C.: Duke University Press, 1947.

De Gaury, G. The New State of Israel. New York: Praeger, 1952.

Dickenstein, A. "Israel's Economic Problems," *Jewish Frontier* (New York), Vol. XVII, No. 7 (July, 1950).

Dunner, J. The Republic of Israel. New York: McGraw-Hill Book Co., Inc., 1950.

Eisenshtadt, S. N. "Le-Darhei Binyan Mangenon ha-Memshalah" (The Ways of Building the Government Machinery), *ha-Arez* (Tel Aviv), 19 Tishrei, 5709: October 22, 1949.

Elston, D. R. "Arabs in Israel," *Israel and Middle East* (Tel Aviv), Vol. III, Nos. 1-2 (January–March, 1951).

Esco Foundation for Palestine. Palestine: A Study of Jewish, Arab and British Policies. New Haven: Yale University Press, 1947.

Federbush, S. "Malchut u-Srarah be-Yisrael" (Sovereignty and Power in Israel), *ha-Doar* (New York), 13 Nisan, 5710: April 30, 1950.

Feldman, S. B. " 'Al Shilton ha-Mishpat ha-'Ivri ba-Medinah" (On the Rule of Hebrew Law in the State), *ha-Hed* (Jerusalem), 24th year, No. 9 (Sivan 5709: June, 1949).

Freiman, A. H. Seder Qidushin we-Nisuin (The Order of Betrothal and Marriage). Jerusalem: Mosad ha-Rav Kook, 1945.

Freiman, A. H. "Ha-Taqanot ha-Hadashot Shel ha-Rabanut ha-Rashit" (The New Rules of the Chief Rabbinate), *Sinai* (Jerusalem), 7th year, Nos. 10-11 (1943).

Friedrich, Karl I. " 'Al Huqat Medinat Yisrael" (On the Constitution of the State of Israel), *Molad* (Tel Aviv Mapai), Vol. II, No. 10 (Tevet, 5709: January, 1949).

Gepstein, S. "Behirot we-Demoqratiah" (Elections and Democracy), *ha-Boker* (Tel Aviv), 15 Av, 5708: August 20, 1948.

Goadby, F. M. International and Inter-Religious Private Law in Palestine. Jerusalem: Hamadpis, 1926.

Goldman, J. "Child Marriages," *Jewish Horizon* (New York), Vol. 12, No. 10 (1950).

Greenberg, H. "Notes on the Israeli Constitution," *Jewish Frontier* (New York), Vol. XVI, No. 5 (May, 1949).

Greenberg, H., ed. Dat Yisrael u-Medinat Yisrael (The Religion of Israel and the State of Israel). New York: Jewish Agency, 1951.

Grossman, M. "Unity in Revisionist Ranks," *Zionist Record* (Johannesburg), Vol. XLIII, No. 1384 (February 2, 1951).

Hanna, Paul L. British Policy in Palestine. Washington: American Council on Public Affairs, 1942.

Hilv, K. "Die Grundlagen der Rechtsentwicklung in Palestine" (The Foundation of Legal Development in Palestine), *Palestina* (Vienna), XVth year, January–February, 1932.

———. "Dat u-Medinah" (Religion and State), *ha-Boker* (Tel Aviv), 15 Av, 5708: August 20, 1948.

———. "Ha-Mishtar ha-Mishpati ba-Medinah ha-Ivrit" (The Legal Order in the Hebrew State), *be-Terem* (Tel Aviv), 21 Adar II, 5708: April 1, 1948.

Hiram, A. "The Communist Party of Israel," *Jewish Frontier* (New York), Vol. XVII, No. 7 (July, 1951).

Hoffman, A. "Rabbinical Courts in Israel," *Jewish Horizon* (New York), June, 1950.

Hurewitz, J. C. The Struggle for Palestine. New York: W. W. Norton & Co., 1950.

Infeld, Z. The Jewish State in the Making. Issued by the Cultural Department of the South African Zionist Federation. Johannesburg: L. E. Joseph & Co., Ltd., n.d.

Intrilligator, David. "The Place of Hapoel Hamizrachi in the Working Community," *Hagesher* (Jerusalem), Vol. III, No. 23-24.

Katzburg, N. "Al ha-Huqah li-Mdinat Yisrael" (On the Constitution for the State of Israel), *Sheluhot* (Jerusalem), No. 6, Av, 5709.

Konvitz, M. "The Bill of Rights in the Draft Constitution for Israel," *The Reconstructionist* (New York), Vol. XIV, No. 20 and No. 21 (February 4 and February 18, 1949).

Kramer, M. "Al Huqat Yisrael" (On the Constitution of Israel), *ha-Arez* (Tel Aviv), 20 Elul, 5708: September 24, 1949.

Krug, Mark M. "Education for Disunity," *Congress Weekly* (New York), Vol. XVI, No. 29 (November 14, 1949).

Landsberg, A. "Ha-Tnu'ah ha Progresivit" (On the Progressive Movement), *ha-Arez* (Tel Aviv), 10 Marheshvan, 5709: November 12, 1948.

Laserson, E. "How is Israel Governed," *New Palestine* (New York), May, 1950.

Lehrman, H. Israel: The Beginning and To-morrow. New York: Wm. Sloane, 1951.

———. "The Israelis Learn to Govern Themselves," *Commentary* (New York), Vol. VIII, No. 1 (July, 1949).

Lewin, Y. Material for the Preparation of a Constitution for the Jewish State on a Religious Basis. New York: Research Institute for Post-War Problems of Religious Jewry, 1948.

Liebenstein, Eli'ezer. "Israel's Social Order," *Congress Weekly* (New York), Vol. XVII, No. 15 (April 24, 1950).

Lu-ah ha-Arez (ha-Arez Calendar). Tel Aviv: Hayyim Pub. Ltd., 5711: 1950.

Maimon, J. L. Hidush ha-Sanhedrin be-Medinateinu ha-Mehudeshet (The Revival of the Sanhedrin in Our Revived State). Jerusalem: Mosad ha-Rav Kook, 5711.

Malik, S., and M. Nurock. "Takhnit ha-Behinot le-'Ovdei Medinat Yisrael" (The Examinations Program for Servants of the State of Israel), *ha-Minahel* (Tel Aviv), No. 5, Spring 1951.

Million, E. M., and A. S. Katz. "Provisions on Religious Freedom in the Draft Israeli Constitution—A Comparative Study," *New York University Law Quarterly Review*, No. 24 (1949).

Nortman, P. Bernard. "Planning Israel's Economic Future," *Jewish Horizon* (New York), Vol. XII, No. 7 (March, 1950).

Or, Menahem. "Ha-Histadrut ha-Ziyonit we-ha-Medinah ha-Ivrit" (The Zionist Federation in the Hebrew State), *be-Terem* (Tel Aviv), 4 Shevat, 5708: January 15, 1948.

Or, Menahem. "Ha-Mishpat bi-Mdinat Yisrael" (Law in the State of Israel), *ha-Boker* (Tel Aviv), 29 Elul, 5708: October 3, 1948.

Palestine Yearbooks. 3 vols. 1946, 1947, and 1948. New York: Zionist Organization of America, 1949.

Pearlman, M. The Army of Israel. New York: Philosophical Library, 1950.

Rackman, E. "The American *vs.* Israeli Rabbinate," *Jewish Horizon* New York), Vol. XIII, No. 6 (1951).

Rosen, Zev. "Le-Mivneh ha-Medinah u-Mangenonah" (The Structure of the State and Her Machinery), *be-Terem* (Tel Aviv), Elul, 5708: September, 1948.

Rosmarin, Trude Weiss. "Israel and the Diaspora," *Jewish Spectator* (New York), Vol. XIV, No. 11 (October, 1949).

Rotenshtreikh, Natan. "Huqah le-Yisrael, ha-Higi'a Shatah" (A Constitution for Israel—Has Its Time Come), *Molad* (Tel Aviv), No. 15 (Sivan, 5709: June, 1949).

Samuel, Edwin. "Israel's Administrative Problems," *Zionist Quarterly* (New York), Vol. I, No. 3 (Winter 1952).

Scheftelowitz, E. Jewish Law of Family and Inheritance. Tel Aviv: Feuchtwanger, 1947.

Schmorak, E. Establishment of the Central Control Office of the World Zionist Organization and the Jewish Agency for Palestine. Submitted to General Zionist Council, Jerusalem, 1947.

Shapiro, I. "Yuqam Bet-Sefer Meuhad be-Yisrael" (Let There Be Established a Unified School in Israel), *ha-Arez,* 26 Tishrei, 5710: October 19, 1949.

Shmuel, Aryeh. "Huqat ha-Medinah ha-Ivrit" (The Constitution of the Hebrew State), *be-Terem* (Tel Aviv), 4 Adar II, 5708: March 15, 1948.

Shragai, S. Z. "Fundamentals of a Torah State," *Jewish Horizon* (New York), Vol. XII, No. 9 (May, 1950), and *Igeret la-Golah* (Jerusalem), No. 24 (May, 1950).

Stein, I. "Why is the Israeli Coalition Government Against a Constitution," *Undzer Weg* (New York: Ahdut-Avodah), 25th year, No. 2 (January 15, 1950).

Stephens, John. "Israel's Economic Progress," *Foreign Commerce Weekly* (New York), Vol. XL, No. 13 (September, 1950).

Toshav, A. "Ha-Tesisah ba-Miflagot" (The Ferment in the Parties), *ha-Doar,* 17 Adar I, 5711: February 23, 1951.

Una, M. "Mi-Saviv ha-Kneset bi-Shelat ha-Huqah" (About the Kneset on the Question of the Constitution), *Netiva* (Tel Aviv), 26th year, No. X.

Wa'ad Leumi. Local Government in Palestine. Memorandum submitted to the United Nations Special Committee on Palestine, 1947.

Wahrhaftig, Z. "Legal Problems in the State of Israel," *Igeret la-Golah* (Jerusalem), November–December, 1949.

Weinryb, B. D. The Yishuv in Palestine. New York: Hadassah, n.d.

Winograd, D. "Tenu'at ha-No'ar ha-Oved we-ha-Palmah" (The Labor Youth Movement and the Palmach), *ha-Ma'aleh* (Tel Aviv: Histadrut), Vol. XVIII, Nos. 11-12 (June 14, 1938).

Zidon, A. Ha-Kneset (The Kneset). Tel Aviv: Amir, 5710.

Zilberg, M. "Bayat ha-Mazav ha-Ishi ba-Mishpat ha-Arzi Yisraeli" (The Issue of Personal Status in the Law of the Land of Israel), *Qovez Harzaot u-Wikuhim* (Jerusalem: Histadrut 'Orhei ha-Din ha-Yehudim, 1938).

———. "Ha-Mishpat ba-Medinah ha-Ivrit" (Law in the Hebrew State), *be-Terem* (Tel Aviv), 21 Shevat, 5708: February 1, 1948.

Zionist Organization of America. Parties in Israel: Their History and Programs. Pamphlet No. 6, n.d.

There are cited in this volume not only the aforementioned books, pamphlets, and essays but also a representative number of editorials from Israel's newspapers and periodicals. The following are published in Tel Aviv: *'Al ha-Homah, 'Al ha-Mishmar, ha'Arez, ha-Boker, Inside Israel, ha-Oved ha-Ziyoni, ha-Poel ha-Ziyoni,* and *be-Terem.* Three others are published in Jerusalem: *Israel Economist, Zion,* and *Zionist Newsletter.* Also cited are cable dispatches of the Jewish Telegraphic Agency.

Index

Index

D

Bei Fragen zur Produktsicherheit wenden Sie sich bitte an:
If you have any questions regarding product safety,
please contact:

Walter de Gruyter GmbH
Genthiner Straße 13
10785 Berlin
productsafety@degruyterbrill.com